T5-AEW-504

TRANSFORMED

TRANSFORMED

BEHIND THE SCENES
WITH **BILLY GRAHAM**

Helen W. Kooiman

Tyndale House Publishers, Wheaton, Illinois
Coverdale House Publishers Ltd., Eastbourne and London, England
Distributed in Canada by Home Evangel Books, Ltd., Ontario, Canada

Library of Congress Catalog Card Number 70-112663
SBN 8423-7300-4
Printed in U.S.A.

Dedicated to Dr. Sherwood E. Wirt,
without whose encouragement and help
this book would never have been written;
and to the thousands involved in
this spiritual adventure, known
and unknown to the author, whose prayers
and labors of love brought
the Crusade at Anaheim into reality.

Contents

Acknowledgements

I am deeply indebted to the Billy Graham Evangelistic Association for giving me the privilege of writing this Anaheim Crusade story, and, in particular, to Dr. Graham who conveyed his approval that the ten days be recorded in this way; and also to Dr. Sherwood E. Wirt and Dr. and Mrs. Walter Smyth whose encouragement made this book possible; and to Dr. George Wilson for meeting with representatives of Tyndale House Publishers and myself to discuss the merits of this book and to add his approval.

Other Team members who responded with helpful suggestions and information were the Rev. Harry Williams, Dr. Robert O. Ferm, Lee Fisher, Willis Haymaker, Cliff Barrows, Mr. and Mrs. George Beverly Shea, Dr. Grady Wilson, Gil Stricklin, Keith Jesson, Bob Jones, John Rogers, The Kinsfolk, Tedd Smith, Carey Moore, and Ake Lundberg.

Thanks also to Dr. and Mrs. Graham's lovely daughter Bunny, and her fiancé at the time — now her husband — Ted Dienert; and to the indefatigable Millie (Mrs. Fred) Dienert for her love and sharing.

Very special gratitude to Mayor Lorin Griset and his wife

Dorothy; Earl and Mary Ann Mooney; Ed and Thelma Elfstrom; Ray and Thelma Smith; Hamp and Sue Riley; Warren and Marj Chartrand; Janet Lawhead; Dara Woodard; Jane Rozelle; Dr. Dave Messenger; Dr. and Mrs. James B. Sheets; Mrs. Frank Pittman; Warren Pittman; the Rev. Robert H. Schuller; the Rev. Galal Gough; the Rev. Armin Gesswein; the Rev. Arvid Carlson; the Rev. Paul Johnson; the Rev. Dick Murray; the Rev. H. E. Jones; the Rev. Kenneth Thengvall; the Rev. Wes Roberts; the Rev. Delbert F. Hosteller; the Rev. Kenneth A. Reeves; and the Rev. William L. Stone.

For her help in supplying stories, thank you to Pam Thompson; and to the newspapers of L.A. and Orange Counties for their outstanding coverage, with particular thanks to Bob Norek and Clay Miller.

Contributing greatly with insight into the volunteer and office work were Bruce and Tone Ferry; Irma Jean Van Roekel; Beverly Giese; Twila Knaack; Karen Lewis; Linda Baker; Marty Lonsdale; Kaleen Ladd; and Jessica Shaver.

To Rick and his dear mother — how I praise God for the two of you! And to Lionel Mayell and the many other counselors and advisors who shared and cared, profoundest thanks. There are literally scores of people who contributed to this book who cannot be named, but for all your interest and prayers my heartfelt gratitude.

Then to Co-Labor Chief Don Myers and his dear wife Sue, and to his captains and their wives — you have a lasting place in my heart!

And last, but certainly not least — some of my greatest indebtedness is to the people at Tyndale House who saw me through this undertaking with wise counsel, invaluable assistance, and huge quantities of patience, love, and understanding. I am referring to sales manager Bob Hawkins, editor Ted Miller, and to publisher Ken Taylor and his wife and family for opening their home and hearts to me.

In a very real sense this is not a book which one person has authored, but it is the work of the thousands who were a part of God's ten days at Anaheim Stadium. Yet this book has just scratched the surface of what is going on as a result of the Anaheim Crusade — a continuing story. What wonderful memories we have of this event, the consequences of which will last for all eternity!

Like Abraham's servant of old, I would say, "I being in the way, the Lord led me . . ." (Genesis 24:27b). May these stories of transformed lives be a transforming experience for many readers.

— HELEN W. KOOIMAN

Wild Wheels

Standing at the bay window in her living room, Mrs. C. drew aside the draperies and paused, watching, waiting, wondering. *Where is Rick? When will he come home?* In the dim light of the hanging lamp she glanced at the wall clock. It was early morning already. She paced the floor. *If only he weren't so crazy about motorcycles. If only he had different friends. If only . . . if only . . . if only . . .*

How many times had she watched and waited, worrying about her son. She wondered if he were lying in a ditch somewhere. What if he'd been in an accident? *Was he — was he on drugs?* The thought caused her to gasp, catching an anguished cry in her throat. When had Rick first begun to make her anxious? Was it four years ago . . . four long years?

The wind felt good against Rick's face. He gave his bike full throttle and surged ahead. His bubble glasses protected his eyes against the wind. The black leather of his jacket glistened as it caught the reflection of the passing cars. This was his bag.

Already at nineteen he had his honorary wings from the

Hell's Angels. Until he was twenty-one he'd work at perfecting his biker skills. Not a stunter in the valley could match his tricks. Who else could spin a motorcycle around at eighty miles an hour — yeah, turn it around and go the opposite way in about fifteen feet! That's where he got his club name Schizo. Everybody called him crazy for doing this stuff. The other bikers, his partners, said he had guts . . . lots of guts. Sometimes he wondered why he attempted these idiotic things. Wondered and hated himself for it.

He revved his engine. Cut out that thinking, softie! But his mother . . . why think about your mother now? Hollywood Boulevard lay dead ahead. He was supposed to meet Deacon and Beast.*

There they were. He hoped a lot of the gang would be showing up, just in case of trouble. It was getting to the point of survival of the fittest among the bikers. Nobody wants to have his teeth kicked in. The Aces would stick together.

How well he remembered what had happened the last time he came down to Hollywood Boulevard. That's when he'd had his Mohawk haircut and was wearing one earring. He couldn't remember whether the guy belonged to the Gypsy Jokers or the Jokers out of Hell — whichever, he was a mean one. A karate expert with two sticks. Those sticks were what got him. Man, had he taken a beating! Cuts, bruises, and scars all over by the time they got done. His mouth was swollen like a watermelon, his eyes bugged out like oranges. That was one guy who could really poke and hit where it hurt. Even so, he had put the karate expert in the hospital. By the time the police arrived he was banging the guy's head against a telephone pole. Was that the time he'd used his belt on his head too? A three-inch-wide strip of Harley Davidson chain made a good weapon. Wonder what ever happened to that guy. Man, that must've hurt. It wasn't really very satisfying. Going soft again, thinking like that. He pulled alongside his friends, the cycle belching its protest.

---

*Some of the names of people in this book have been changed at their request or the discretion of the publisher.

"Hey, man, I heard you tested George's bike the other day . . ." Beast was the first to greet him.

He'd almost forgotten, but how could he? "Yep! Harley Davidson with a springer front end and a Corvair car engine. Had it up to 135 — goin' pretty fast, man . . ."

"Where'd you do it?" Deacon could hardly believe his ears.

"Benedict Canyon . . . long ways out. What are we waitin' for?"

"Charlie's got a quarter of stuff — pure heroin this time. We're supposed to come over and help cut it and balloon it."

"Man, let's get going. I can use some of that." Rick gunned his engine and the others joined him.

He was mainlining now. It had begun with marijuana. He was a biker and bikers stuck to this stuff. The hippies were something else. They scared him, the way some of them took Speed. He wasn't about to get strung out on some of those hard drugs. Shoot Methedrine straight for three weeks and, man, you could die. He wasn't ready to die . . . that bothered him. He hoped he'd have sense enough to remember that when he got going on a "trip" — he hoped he'd remember to stay off his bike.

A guy could get in trouble with the fuzz over this stuff. If the law got on your heels, man, watch out! OK, so he'd been caught a few times, but never on anything they could pin him with or hold him for long. One couldn't be too careful, though. If he were twenty-one he'd already have a one-percenter patch, the honor patch worn by "outlaw" bikers. He'd broken the law all right, but he had to reach twenty-one to qualify for the patch. People say it's easy to be bad. Well, it isn't, if they only knew. It's easy to be normally bad, but to be extremely bad when you don't want to be — no, he really didn't want to do all this stuff. Why did he?

As they zoomed along, Rick's mind was playing tricks on him. It bothered him — these questions coming up all the time. He needed a shot. What day was this? Sunday. Sunday, September 28. He needed a "trip." He'd be OK after some acid.

2

Gold Seekers

California is not just California; it is a collection of states and people from across the country. Each evening as the sun sets over the Pacific there are at least fifteen hundred more people in the state than the day before. Some six hundred of these are newborn babies — the rest are migrating Americans answering the siren song of the Golden West. Since James Marshall discovered gold at Sutter's Mill on the American River near Sacramento on January 24, 1848, folks have been seeking their fortune where the warm sun meets the gentle Pacific.

In the hearts of the thousands who come, there is hope. It may be a wispy hope, but it's real. They are people who are not afraid to live by their wits. In this respect they are not so different from their wagon-train predecessors. They are Americans on the go. They're not finding the millennium in California, but the statistics indicate they are finding the life enough better so that they do not care to move back. Many do return east for a year or so, only to move to California permanently after another winter in their former home. The lure of the Golden West is compelling, for it is a beautiful and delightful part of the world. Climate is a factor; much of California is virtually seasonless. Evenings are usually cool. In the summertime one need never worry about mosquitoes. You can leave your snow shovel behind when you move west, unless you choose to live in the mountains. Cabrillo, a navigator of great courage and honor, explored California in 1542 and called it a "land of endless summers." After four hundred years it still is!

California is a big state with big problems. Sexual emancipation was first exploited by the California movie cameras. Campus anarchy broke out first in this state. Topless and bottomless entertainers made their first appearance in California cities. The largest agriculture strike in history took root in California. According to the FBI's J. Edgar Hoover, California is also the first state in crime.

Who causes the big problems? California is kin to the rest of the nation. People cause the problems, and aggressive individualists have been drawn to the state along with ordinary folk and those who are considered "nuts." Are the people of California so different from people in other parts of the country? A *Ladies' Home Journal* article put it like this: "The frontier has always attracted the desperate and the unstable, and California has more than its share of both types."

Southern California is a slice of life, a smorgasbord of the good and bad. Where else can you find slums with palm trees? In southern California everything seems more open, more possible, more available. The region is crowded with canyons that have been subdivided and paved and ridges that have been leveled in what has been called a "superb triumph" of earthmoving technology. Examples of landscape butchery abound. Housewives periodically rise in revolt against the bulldozers, but what can they do? New people need a place to live.

Californians are more prosperous and leisure minded, own more telephones, drive more than 10 percent of the national total of automobiles, and possess more of everything than most states in the country. They joke about their blinding, suffocating, citywide smog. There is a transitory feeling that can be unsettling to the newcomer — if he allows himself time to think about it, that is. Speaking of time, most people would rather not! One writer has said, "You don't need to give us time. We don't use it. It is tomorrow already in California. Keep moving along there, buddy, your seat is up front."

Into this microcosm of affluent, harried America came a bright spot on the smoggy horizon in early 1968. Not all Californians are restless. Not all are geared to high-pressure, pleasure-seeking drives. There are also the concerned, the patient, the praying, and those who are motivated by love. These solid folk know that California is basically little different from other parts of the country. The Golden State has no monopoly on problems. I came to California from Iowa, and my friends and relatives in the Midwest assure me they are well supplied with headaches of their own. We are a nation — from East Coast to West — who too often have left God out of our activities — and now we can't handle them.

Some Christians in southern California who were moved by love, and who were aware of the great needs of people searching for an illusive something they could not define, talked about the possibility of bringing Evangelist Billy Graham to speak to their condition. The talking culminated in the opening of a Crusade office in Anaheim in the fall of 1968.

Why Anaheim? What did Anaheim offer that an evangelistic crusade required? To mention the first — and foremost — requirement, Anaheim had praying people who were yearning to see the power of God displayed. God was ready to answer.

3

Pause to Pray

"Super-America" is the name hung on southern California. They weren't calling it that a hundred years ago; in fact, you couldn't have found a daily newspaper, a railroad, an evangelical church, or even a theater or concert hall in those parts in 1865. It is difficult to imagine the bustling megalopolis of Los Angeles as a small, sleepy town clustered around a plaza church, a saloon, and several stores, fringed on the west and south by the beautiful blue Pacific; but that's the way it was. As late as 1943 the Los Angeles area had no freeways, no TV aerials, no jet airplanes, no giant airport, no music center, no electronics or space industries, no Disneyland, and no smog.

No Disneyland? In the minds of young America, Disneyland seems to have existed always. Residents of Orange County are used to the hails of tourists: "How do we get to Disneyland?" The automatic answer: "Straight ahead to Anaheim." Writing in *The Saturday Review,* Myron Roberts described Orange County as "the fastest growing, most affluent county in the most affluent state in the most affluent country in the history of the world." And what of Anaheim? This fast-growing neighbor of Los Angeles prides itself on attractions for international travelers, American convention-goers, and local fun-seekers. The city lies at the hub of the sprawling complex known as Orange County, commercially famous as "the happiest place on earth"—the site of Walt Disney's Magic Kingdom.

With ten million visitors a year swarming over its 70 acres of park entertainment, Disneyland's impact on the surrounding area is immense. A great new tourist, convention, and entertainment business has sprung up since 1950. Anaheim, the center of it all, sits astride the famed Santa Ana Freeway, main connecting artery between Los Angeles some twenty-five miles to the northwest, and San Diego seventy-five miles to the south. That freeway and others in the surrounding area were to be jammed nightly during the ten days of the Crusade as thousands converged into the area.

A few hundred yards away from Disneyland lies the $20 million Anaheim Stadium, home of the California Angels Baseball Club and site of the Billy Graham Crusade. The Angels had been struggling to climb out of the nether regions of the American League's western division. On September 24 they played their final game of the season and made way for other "angels," the invisible variety that, Scripture tells us, inhabit the heavens and sometimes dip low on missions of mercy for their Lord.

On Thursday evening, September 25, 1969, a new moon peeped through the nighttime haze, but it attracted few observers among the crowd gathering at Anaheim Stadium. It was dedication night for the Graham Crusade, and at 7:23 a massive choir sang out in unison: "Praise ye the Lord of hosts, Sing of His salvation . . ." Attention was riveted on a wooden platform behind the pitcher's mound where songleader Cliff Barrows directed the singers and Tedd Smith performed piano magic.

Jack L. Coleman, well-known choral conductor and composer, surveyed the scene with a prayer of thanksgiving. Many months previously Mayor Lorin Griset of Santa Ana, chairman of the Crusade executive committee, had invited him to assume responsibility for recruiting and training five thousand singers from churches throughout southern California. It was a formidable assignment, but Coleman was no stranger to musical challenges. In March 1969 he became choral director for the "King Family Show" on the NBC-TV network. For four years he had served as choral master for the world-famous Laguna Festival of Opera in Laguna Beach. Now Coleman shook his head in amazement as the voices swelled. Were there really nearly eight thousand people in that choir? He remembered another scene twenty years earlier when he had sung in a Gospel quartet for a flamboyant ex-Fuller Brush salesman-turned-college president and evangelist. Yes, that was Billy Graham too.

A capacious tent at Washington Boulevard and Hill Street in Los Angeles is known to history as the place where Billy Graham launched his first major evangelistic Crusade in the United States. The event was called "The Christ for Greater Los Angeles Campaign." Billy was dubbed by a newspaperman as "Gabriel in gabardine," a label that he wore with a blush. He was young, flashy, with a zeal and charm that caught the attention of some of the Hollywood celebrities — cowboy radio singer Stuart Hamblen, track star Louis Zamperini, and the syndicate-hired electronics wizard Jim Vaus.

The night Stuart Hamblen walked forward to declare his faith in Christ, a maid employed at the San Simeon castle of publisher William Randolph Hearst was in the audience. She knew her boss was a Hamblen fan and she reportedly told him what had happened. The next day Hearst sent a two-word telegram to the managing editor of the *Los Angeles Examiner*: "PUFF GRAHAM."

Hearst's editors splashed the evangelist's story across their Sunday pages. To this day Graham will tell you that whatever happened, he believes it was of God. And today Billy Graham is news wherever he goes, whether to Paris, Berlin, London, Nairobi, Saigon, Addis Ababa, Rio de Janeiro, Prague — or Anaheim.

Cliff Barrows's voice penetrated Jack Coleman's thoughts. "Our purpose tonight is to dedicate first of all ourselves, and then these facilities to the glory of God for the next ten days. Let's lift our hearts together in praise and sing, 'All Hail the Power of Jesus' Name' . . ."

Afterward the Reverend Robert H. Schuller, vice-chairman of the local Crusade committee, prayed:

"O God, You are our refuge and strength, our very present help,
O God, You are our power and our life.
O God, You have a beautiful and a big dream for the redemption of the lives of men in this place;
Take, we pray, O Holy Spirit, every life, beginning with mine, every person in this place;
Make us clean in mind and heart.
O God, we pray now a special blessing on Billy, Cliff, Tedd — every member of this team,
Strength to their hearts and physical bodies;
Holy Spirit, empower them that their words might reach deeply into the hearts of men;
O God, tomorrow night this place will be filled with Your Holy Spirit and we are ready to be used.
We await You prayerfully,
In Your name, Amen."

Mayor Griset then opened his heart: "For five years we have been looking forward to the event that is now upon us. This morning Mr. Graham addressed sixteen hundred businessmen and civic leaders at Convention Center. Afterward one man told me, 'Up to this point my Christianity has been characterized by an effort to live by the Golden Rule. Lorin, I've been wrong. It's not enough. From now on I'm going to trust Jesus Christ; I'm going to depend on Him alone.'

"We are already seeing what God is going to do through this Crusade. We need to invite our friends because we have God's men leading us. It's thrilling to be identified with men who have put Jesus Christ right in the center of their lives. We are expecting God to make southern California a better place in which to live. Let's continue to pray for one another and work together so that God can use all of us."

Harry Williams, southern California Crusade Director, stepped to the mike. "It seems incredible that so many months have gone so fast, and so many hundreds of people have become involved. The result is expressed by this great choir, by all the ushers, counselors, advisors, and workers who are gathered. I, along with you, am very excited, encouraged, and thankful to God for what He has done behind the scenes. Some eight thousand people have attended the Christian Life and Witness classes and over four thousand people the Bible study series in preparation for follow-up. This represents nearly five hundred churches throughout southern California. Now we are ready to receive the fruit of the labor night after night in this great stadium."

During the dedication I stood on the playing field with four Team members: Dr. Robert O. Ferm, long-time consultant to Billy Graham; Dr. Sherwood Wirt, editor of Graham's *Decision* magazine; Willis Haymaker, Crusade organizer and "elder statesman" of the Team; and Ake Lundberg, *Decision* photographer.

Marveling at this vast choir, Willis Haymaker said, "This choir is starting where the 1963 Los Angeles Crusade choir left off!" Haymaker was Graham's first Crusade director, setting up and supervising Crusades across the country and around the world.

Cliff Barrows opened his Bible and read from 2 Chronicles: "If my people, which are called by my name, shall humble themselves, and pray, and seek my face, and turn from their wicked ways; then will I hear from heaven, and will forgive their sin, and will heal their land."

Beside me, Mr. Haymaker whispered: "That is God's blueprint for spiritual awakening."

Cliff went on: "Here is a promise we can claim this evening. This stadium will be an open air cathedral where God will be worshiped in song and in spoken word; and you, as workers, will determine in great measure the atmosphere of this place. This will be God's house. Let us walk humbly and softly before Him. And then let us believe Him that through our lives He will do something we never dreamed possible. There is no better time for revival to begin than in our own hearts, right here tonight. Let's ask God to meet our needs, and then through our lives overflow into the lives of others."

Cliff's prayer of dedication was a solemn moment for everyone: "We pray You will continue to do Your work and by the Holy Spirit reveal to us not only our need of You in a new way, but the glorious fact that You are able to supply every need we have. We pray that Your Holy Spirit will empower us for service in every function You have called us to fulfill. And so we dedicate these facilities to You. We dedicate our lives afresh to You. We pray that each of us, as we come to sing, to usher, to counsel, to work and help, that the lives of countless numbers of people, not only here but throughout America, may be blessed and changed as they share by television in this Crusade."

A few days earlier, in a pre-crusade prayer meeting, I had heard neighbors and friends asking God for these same blessings. Along with others I had prayed and worked for the opening of this Crusade, never dreaming I'd have the privilege of going behind the scenes of the Crusade and then of being asked to write a book about God's marvelous working. From my home in Fullerton a few miles north of Anaheim, I can see the glow of the giant "A" as it pierces the night sky at the stadium. Now as the Crusade Team, the local leaders, and the workers filed out of the stadium, the towering "A" with its halo of light seemed to signal a great "Amen."

4

Spotlight on the Pitcher

People came by plane, bus, train, and car to Anaheim Stadium, some from as far away as Nova Scotia and Alaska. Chartered groups traveled from Oregon, Nevada, Arizona, Utah, and even Tennessee, some five hundred delegations arriving during the Crusade. They belonged to breakfast clubs, civic organizations, women's societies, youth groups, and churches. Industrious Bob Jones of the Crusade office saw that the delegations got reserved seats in the stadium.

From all over the southland they arrived. As for the local populace, it seemed to turn out en masse. Churches had been encouraged to give half of their bus space to friends unaffiliated with a church, and many did. From the stadium's second level, buses could be seen rolling into the mammoth parking area from all directions. One night 400 buses were counted.

The audience ranged from babes in arms, contentedly sucking on bottles, to the aged who needed canes or friends' arms for support. The ages in between represented California's variegated populace: carefree in party and work clothes, moccasins and sandals and bare feet, bell-bottom slacks and miniskirts and even furs.

California's Governor Ronald Reagan rose from his platform chair among the honored guests and Team members on opening night. "I'm sure there will be those who question my participation here tonight," he said. "People have become so conscious of the separation of church and state that we have interpreted freedom of religion to be freedom from religion. . . .

"On the deck of the tiny ship *Arbella* in the year 1630, John Winthrop reminded a little band of Puritans that the eyes of all people would be upon them, and if they dealt falsely with God and the work He had given them they would indeed be sorry.

"I would remind you," said the governor, "that there is no need in our land today greater than the need to rediscover our spiritual heritage. Many nations have exchanged their gods for new gods, but no nation has exchanged its god for no god at all and lived to add any further pages to history.

"Our young people today cry out for a cause — a belief in which they can invest their youthful strength. Too often the cause they find is tragically false. In one year, runaway young people from all across this land have come to one of our California cities, San Francisco. I don't know exactly what they were seeking, but I know what they found. A total of 2,056 were questioned in one year in narcotic investigations, 1,731 were jailed, 4,692 were treated in one hospital alone for narcotic poisoning and bad trips, 2,613 were treated for VD, 861 mothered illegitimate and unsupported children, 3,280 underage delinquents were arrested for mugging, burglaries, and shoplifting, 26 were murdered.

"Why is a representative of government here in a gathering of this kind? To welcome with humble pride a man whose mission in life has been to remind us that in all our confusion the answer to each and every problem can be found in the simple words of Jesus of Nazareth who urged us to love one another.

"The man we welcome here by word and example can show even the most turned-off in our turned-off society that this is where the action really is. I have no words to express my pleasure in having the privilege on behalf of fellow Californians of welcoming to our state the Reverend Billy Graham. We bid you welcome and tell you that we need to hear what you are going to say."

Several notable personalities followed Governor Reagan to the platform on various nights. Ethel Waters, Norma Zimmer, Myrtle Hall, and, of course, George Beverly Shea sang their testimonies, and Miss California of 1968 and Los Angeles Ram gridder Maxie Baughan spoke theirs.

The burly footballer told the audience: "It's hard to live like we know we should live. It's hard for Maxie Baughan to do that today — to live a Christian life. But we're not asked to die, we're asked to live, and with the love of Christ in our hearts it can be done."

Sharon Kay Terrill, Miss California of 1968, had viewed the beauty contest with surprising depth of vision. She told the Crusade audience: "One can be a beauty queen and a Christian, too. God's plan really unfolded itself to me when I found that I wanted to do God's will more than I wanted to win. Winning was important, but accepting Christ and following His plan more so."

In high school Sharon Kay had considered herself a Christian, she said, but Christianity seemed a bore. Her goal was to live an exciting life. Then in college Sharon Kay met a girl who told her God loved her and had a wonderful plan for her life. Sharon Kay discovered God's plan was much more exciting than anything she could attain by herself.

The final test question for the California contestants was: "What is the most important attribute parents can give their children?" Sharon Kay breathed a little prayer, then answered: "A spiritual relationship with Jesus Christ." She wondered momentarily if she had "blown it" with a pious answer, but the wondering was short-lived for she soon received the crown of Miss California.

Perhaps the greatest audience response to a guest speaker came after a testimony by a young Marine Corps officer, a veteran of the war in Vietnam. Lt. Clebe McClary held his New Testament between the steel clamps of his artificial left arm and scanned the quiet audience with his good eye as he told of a strict South Carolina upbringing. "My dad said, 'Clebe, you go to church,' and Clebe went to church!" He described the night battle in Vietnam when he and his troops came under enemy attack. Only a few were lifted out alive by 'copter. The sixteen surgical operations he endured had helped to restore his physical powers, but now he spoke of the spiritual power he had received since returning home, upon believing in Christ.

The cool evening wind picked up Lt. McClary's words: "We bear allegiance to the flag of our country, but unless we have been born again through faith in Christ, all our religion is worth nothing." When he stepped down from the podium, the crowd stood to its feet and applauded spiritedly for minutes, many people with tears in their eyes.

Early newspaper reports described the Crusade as a success and noted that the handsome, 50-year-old preacher who was pitching the sermons "wooed youths and rapped intellectuals." A brilliant surgeon, among others, took the rap. He heard Graham say that if gaining heaven depended upon good deeds, the evangelist himself would not expect to get there. The surgeon took the Gospel way, committing his life to Christ with hundreds of others.

5

Tuned-in Youth

The Kinsfolk, a musical group comprising three brothers and a sister from Sydney, Australia, provided the musical attraction for the Crusade youth nights. The moment they made the scene with a unique style of folk singing, the audience responded. Clapping started spontaneously in the third tier of the stadium and swept forward and sideways, a swelling wave of sound.

The Kinsfolk beat was distinctive and the thousands of youth who made up the greater share of the audience were tuned in. The reaction was not surprising to Cliff Barrows or other Team members. Marion, nineteen, Tim, twenty-one, Richard, twenty-five, and Ross Begbie, thirty-one, elicited this kind of response wherever they went. Their singing career began in 1964 as a "self-entertainment" venture, but audience appreciation launched them on an RCA long-playing album in Australia that later landed on U.S. shores.

The Kinsfolk are the first such singing group to join the Billy Graham Team. During their stay in southern California they were constantly on the go, making appearances at Knott's Berry Farm, Disneyland, the Los Angeles County Fair, Christian Businessmen's luncheons and dozens of school, church, and industry assemblies. Fuller Seminary student Keith Jesson, with his delightful New Zealand accent, served as manager for the popular group.

The Begbies obviously are caught up on a strong musical tide. Richard's regular work is that of a vicar in the Church of England, diocese of Sydney; Ross teaches high school music, and writes and arranges most of the Kinsfolk numbers; Tim took a year's leave of absence from the University of Sydney Medical School to play the double bass for the group; and Marion ordinarily teaches kindergarten children. Their songs came through to all ages, tuning hearts for the upbeat message Billy Graham presented . . .

I find that young people everywhere are searching for a purpose. They are searching for a cause to commit themselves to, a flag to follow, a song to sing. You can find it in a personal relationship with Jesus Christ, the Son of the living God!

The third chapter of 2 Timothy reads: "Remember this! There will be difficult times in the last days. For men will be selfish, greedy, boastful, and conceited; they will be insulting, disobedient to their parents, ungrateful, and irreligious; they will be unkind, merciless, slanderers, violent, and fierce; they will hate the good; they will be treacherous, reckless, and swollen with pride; they will love pleasure rather than God; they will hold to the outward form of our religion, but reject its real power."

I heard about a young person who said to his parent when he got angry, "You know, I didn't ask to be born!" And the angry parent retorted, "If you had, the answer would have been 'No.' " Young people of today are the first to grow up with so-called "modern parents." They have grown up with affluence, tremendous social and technological change, and violence. It's the first generation to grow up with television! It's the first generation that's been bombarded from childhood by suggestions of false needs, and the first to create the generation gap . . . and the expectation gap! You have to have all these material things to find fulfillment and happiness.

Who are these young people that we read about? I've tried to get to know some of them. I've met by the hour with some hippies. And I've learned that they're not all that we seem to think they are. I know there are some hard-core radicals, a small, well-organized minority who say they are going to destroy the system. They will not compromise, and they believe that they are winning!

And there are the idealistic: they want to remake society. They know there is social injustice. They are concerned about poverty. They grapple with the race issues. They question the war in Vietnam. They want to do something, but don't know how to go about it. So they lash out in frustration.

A third group riot, demonstrate, and engage in disorders just for kicks. Some cop out and drop out of society because they are failures in school. They rationalize their failure and blame the system instead of themselves.

Well, the Bible teaches the very opposite. The Bible teaches that everyone is a sinner in the sight of God, and everyone is a rebel by nature against God. The whole human race, the Bible tells us, is in rebellion against God! Adam rebelled against God, Cain rebelled against God, the people at the Tower of Babel rebelled against God! Isaiah the prophet quoted God's lament: "I've nourished and brought up children and they rebelled against Me." Rebellion is nothing new. This whole planet is in rebellion against God.

Our little planet, a speck of dust, in rebellion against the great and mighty God! You and I strut around saying, "Look how big we are and how important we are." But we are like ants, living a few days on this earth before entering a mysterious eternity — and boasting how great we are! No wonder the Bible says God laughs and has rulers in derision when they take counsel against Him!

But the Bible teaches that this is also the only planet that Jesus Christ came into, as far as we know. God loves the people of this planet so much that He was willing to give His Son for their salvation. God could have wiped out the rebellious human race, but He said, "I love them; I am not willing that any should perish." And He sent His Son to take our sins and our rebellion and our death and our hell on the cross, because the penalty in God's universe for rebellion against Him is death and hell! On the cross Jesus took the death and the hell that you and I deserve, and said, "I forgive you." More than that: "I am going to give you eternal life, and when you die, your spirit, the real you, is going to heaven to live forever as a son of God in a special relationship that is higher than the angels or any other principalities or powers that exist anywhere in the universe!"

Nobody can possibly comprehend the greatness of the love of God that could take a poor, miserable sinner like me and lift me above the stars, and above the angels, and above principalities and powers, and make me a son of God! That is what happens when you give your life to Jesus Christ!

The big question I find among young people today is this: "What is the purpose and the meaning of my life? How do I find identity?" The Kinsfolk sing "Who is Why? Don't tell me how, tell me why." Nietzsche, an atheist, once said, "If any man has a 'why' for his life, he can bear with almost any 'how.' " If you don't have meaning in your life, it ceases to be worth living.

Why do I have to die? Why do I have to suffer? Why must I struggle? Why am I involved in guilt? Who am I? Where am I going? Many students today are finding higher education almost meaningless. We have ignored those questions in higher education, and students want to know the answer. *The only authoritative answer in the world is this Book — the Word of God!* And that's the reason it's important to read the Bible and study it. Get a modern translation; you may not believe all you read, you may not understand all you read, but read it!

Tolstoy once said that each of us is stuck with a God-shaped blank in our heart. You were born with it, and without God it'll always be blank. And you'll search for happiness and peace and joy but you won't find them — because *they're found ultimately and completely in Christ!*

You won't find them in money, in popularity, in being pretty, in sex — *you'll find them in Christ,* the total, complete, ultimate fulfillment of your life! You were made for God!

How many restless young people are searching, questioning? Oh, on the outside you are one thing, but underneath you are something else. When you get alone and you start thinking, you really want completeness and happiness and joy and purpose and meaning. You can find them in an experience with Jesus Christ! Eugene O'Neill said, "Life's only meaning is death." I say he is wrong! Life can find meaning here and now by a personal relationship with Christ! Do you know Christ? Is He yours?

Give your life to Christ, and let Him set you free! Because, you see, the only free people in all the world are those who know Christ. Everybody else is in bondage to sin. We hear people screaming all over the world: "Freedom! Freedom! Freedom now! Freedom!" Even if they have political freedom, they'll still be in spiritual and moral bondage.

When Jesus Christ died on the cross, He died to provide a righteousness for you, a goodness for you. And God gives it to you as a gift. And the apostle said, "Be clothed in the righteousness of Jesus Christ." I am not going to go to heaven because I have read the Bible and prayed and gone to church or been a preacher. I am going to heaven because I am clothed in righteousness given to me as a free gift by Jesus Christ. I didn't deserve it, but I have spiritual life in me as a free gift from God because of what Christ did on the cross. And you can have the same gift. You receive it by faith! "But as many as received him, to them gave he power to become the sons of God, even to them that believe on his name" . . .

Billy waited quietly while young people and adults began advancing to the platform to express their commitment to Christ. An estimated 60 percent of the crowd was under twenty-five years old. In some cases counselors and inquirers alike were in "mod" attire, presenting as colorful a group as has ever been seen at a Crusade, with their bell-bottom pants, miniskirts, bare feet, long hair, beards, chains, and other adornments.

Southern California has perhaps more hippies than any area of the country, and, as I looked down onto the field from the stadium press box after the service, I realized that many hippie-types were professing Christians.

After the service, a group of Bible-carrying hippies were singing on the field and I decided to find out who they were. As I approached, I heard: "Born, born, born again; Praise God I've been born again . . ."

"What are you doing, and who are you?" I asked.

"We're just a bunch of guys and gals who love Jesus Christ." Most of them were sitting cross-legged on the grass, and they welcomed me with broad, friendly smiles.

A neat-looking fellow joined in, "A lot of these young people attend a church in south Santa Ana. I happen to be a friend of the pastor there. These kids are turned on for Christ."

There was something compelling about these kids; they certainly weren't putting on an act. "Will you tell me why you dress like this? Why the long hair, and why the beards?"

"See that kid over there?" One of them pointed to a very hippyish-looking person. "I'm interested in kids like that and want to spread the words of Christ. God can reach them through me dressed in this way."

I looked at a girl wearing a counselor badge bearing the name "Dottie." "What about you, Dottie? Describe the way you're dressed."

"I have on a long dress, blue-green color, and a blue cape." A hairy purse dangled from her arm as she held tightly to a well-worn Bible. Her granny glasses with their round frames had slipped to the end of her nose.

"What do your parents think about this?" I asked another.

"My parents are very glad that I'm in it, but they're wondering if I'm not getting too deep in it, you know, because I'm so young. My aunt called me a religious fanatic because I believe that you must abide completely by the Bible and not be lukewarm."

Another fellow spoke up. "We have a girl whose mother said she'd rather have her shooting dope than following Christ. We run into a lot of that. It's pretty sad. We know a girl who just accepted Christ, and her family put her into an institution. It's a bad scene. . . ."

"Were you on drugs?" I looked at him intently.

"Yes, ma'am. Most of us were drug users before we surrendered to Christ. Most of us had long hair when we came to Christ, and we had our beards. We looked this way before we came to Christ, but the Lord says He's chosen the foolish things of the world to confound the wise. We realize, even as Mr. Graham realizes, that drugs and sex are some of the biggest problems confronting young people today. They're doing what they call their own thing; trying to run away from God, just like Mr. Graham said tonight. So we're kinda' trying to blend in with them and then witness to them. And you know, it works!"

"Amen!" said one.

"Praise the Lord!" said another.

And Rick, the wild biker, was in the audience Monday night, too, *almost* back from the acid trip he'd taken the night before. I saw Rick from a distance that night, and talked with his tearful mother. I didn't learn much of his story then, but there wasn't much to tell yet; at least, not much of the spiritual trip he was to take from hell's gate to heaven's border. The story, when I learned it all, turned out to be almost as harrowing as Rick's many rides for the devil.

6

Cleansing of Acid Eyes

Rick hadn't wanted to come to the Crusade, but his mother had made up her mind, and what could a guy do? He didn't like the idea of her bucking traffic alone all the way to Anaheim from the San Fernando Valley. What if she had a flat or some other car trouble? Some pothead desperate for dough might give her trouble. No, he'd better go. She was a pretty swell mother. Wonder if she guessed that he was on the stuff. Hope not! And his biking . . . she never mouthed off at him. Wish she wouldn't worry so much. And pray. Why did she have to pray like that?

He looked across the stadium aisle to where his mother sat. Guess he shouldn't have asked her to sit by herself. She looked kinda tired . . . wonder if she waited up for me last night. Wonder what time it was when I got home. Man, my head aches. Wish my eyes didn't burn so . . .

Rick fidgeted restlessly. Wish I could smoke . . . wonder what these people around would think if I lit up. Why don't they stop looking at me? Haven't they ever seen a guy in grubbies before? What's everybody doing? Going forward, are they? Hah! Lot of good it'll do 'em. I should know; I tried that before — doesn't last.

"Rick, do you want to go down?" His mother was by his side.

"No, let's get out of this place."

He hadn't remembered that they'd parked the car so far back in the stadium lot. Made him mad . . . he'd like to kick over all those lane dividers. Who did Graham think he was, anyway, spouting off about heaven and hell and all the other things he said. How's a guy supposed to know if there really was such a place as heaven or hell? Who wants to give up all one's friends and his bike for something you can't be sure about? Girls were great, dope was beautiful — give up these things for Graham's pie-in-the-sky?

Suddenly Rick was shouting profanities into the air. Where was his mother anyway? He waited impatiently for her to catch up and then impulsively started running back toward the stadium, almost as though he were being chased. "I've gotta go back . . . gotta talk to Billy Graham . . . maybe something awful will happen to me tonight if I don't. . . ." His eyes were blinking wildly; his face was pale with a nameless fear.

Mrs. C. turned anxiously and followed her son. She knew Billy Graham would be gone. "O God, have the right people waiting. . . ." she breathed.

Rick was down on the field by the time she caught up. It had been like swimming upstream with all those people coming out of the stadium. She stepped to the side of the playing field. Mustn't let anything interfere . . . stay back. . . .

On the field several counselors were letting Rick empty his heart. He told them his hang-up was that he'd tried to do the things he knew should be done, tried to chuck his bad friends, but it all seemed impossible. He had found drugs, his friends, and his motorcycle more fun than trying to live as a Christian. He doubted Christ's existence. But his real quest was for inner peace, and it seemed he didn't dare leave the stadium without talking out his problems with someone.

John McMullin gripped Rick by the shoulder and urged:

"Rick, come back tomorrow night. I promise you'll see God work miracles in your life. I'll be waiting for you somewhere between the choir and aisle 19. I'll find you . . ."

What John hadn't told Rick was that this section required tickets for entrance. It was one of the areas reserved for those who had received tickets through their church. Rick came again on Tuesday night, marching up jauntily, his mother close behind. When the usher stopped him and asked, "May I see your tickets?" Rick answered, "I'm supposed to meet a counselor between the choir and aisle 19." The usher took a second look at the tall, skinny kid in what were the grubbiest grubbies he'd ever seen, and said, "All right." Behind him the usher was stopping all those who didn't have tickets, directing them to another section of the stadium.

Was it divine appointment? Rick walked directly to where John was sitting. The mother slipped away at Rick's request to sit elsewhere. When she spotted her son again striding out on the field, Billy had finished speaking.

Rick stood in front of the speaker's platform trying to attract the evangelist's attention. People were getting in front of him, blocking his view. He surmised that Billy had left the speaker's platform at the rear. OK, he'd show 'em; he edged his way around, thinking to confront Billy. He failed. A counselor took hold of his arm, talking, holding him back. Rick gave it up and walked back into the stadium, losing himself in the crowd.

On Wednesday evening an inner compulsion made Rick go to the stadium again. John was waiting for him. This time Rick listened intently to the sermon. He heard hell described as an abyss of loneliness. He heard Billy read from a magazine article about a student who took a drug-triggered trip that seemed like a ride into hell. Rick rubbed his eyes. "Acid eyes," the guys called them, and with good reason. Was it Sunday night he'd gone on that LSD trip? Just three nights ago!

Hell . . . that's what it had been like. Lights coming toward you and slamming through you. One of the lights changed into a mouth, like a lion's mouth, and the lights became teeth and opened up wide to swallow you. He shuddered. Graham was telling it straight. What Billy Graham didn't say was what it was like to go on a "bum trip." Rick could tell them. There was a spoon here, and below it another spoon. Below that another, all the way down, one spoon after another. Images, one superimposed upon another.

There was a couch. And another couch, and another. More couches. Then there was the spoon again. A spoon and a couch, another spoon and couch.

He remembered looking up at the ceiling. But now the couch was on the ceiling. And so was the spoon. Ceiling, couches, spoons. It was doubling, and doubling again. Each time his eyes moved he saw more images. His mind felt strained to the breaking point. At that point he "freaked" out. He thought he was going to die. Wished he could. Bum trip!

Preacher, you said it right. Hell!

Billy had finished talking. Rick rose from his seat and again lost John in the crowd. Pushing his way forward, he headed directly for the side of the platform. He had to get to Billy tonight. He stood at the side, looking up, waiting. All of a sudden he was surrounded by men holding his arms. They thought he was trying to harm Billy. Rick could wrap them all around the Big "A" if he wanted to. Why wasn't he fighting like the other times when he got mad? Why was he crying?

Billy had left the field. Rick was free to go. He started running to the edge of the field. A counselor followed, caught hold of his arm and said, "Come on, let's sit down here on the grass and talk." He was gentle. Through blurred eyes Rick regarded him cautiously.

High in the stadium Mrs. C. strained her eyes to see what was happening. Never had her gaze left her son. Never had she prayed harder. Rick left the counselor and headed for the parking lot. Before getting far he began yelling and screaming. In the distance he had heard a train and he headed in the direction of the tracks. "I'll throw myself on the tracks." But he couldn't run fast enough; the train disappeared. Rick's mother hurried to her car, on the way encountering another counselor and his wife. With two cars they began circling through the parking lot. There was no trace of Rick. When she stopped her car the counselor suggested she go back into the stadium. Possibly he had returned.

Everything was dark, but three aisles over from where she stood Mrs. C. made out the figure of her son. With him was another man. She moved back into the shadows; Rick must not be disturbed.

Rick had come back into the stadium, completely unnerved and exhausted. He wanted to yell out, "God can go to hell!" but the words choked in his throat. It was as if God had put a chain around his vocal cords. Lazlo Lak, 30-year-old Hungarian, a music instructor at California State College and a counselor, recalls what happened with Rick. "He came into the stadium very angry. Angry at God. He was rebelling, fighting himself, saying, 'I wish I'd never come here. I'm so disturbed . . . I'm all messed up.' I talked to him for some time, and gradually he quieted down. I suggested to him that he consider that God was working in his heart, causing his turmoil. After a time of talking and sharing with him what God has to say in the Bible, I suggested he go home, rest, and pray, asking God to help him. I reminded him that he must trust God fully. . . ."

Rick left. His face was different. He was calm. Rejoining his mother, he said simply, "Let's go home."

When Mrs. C. left for work on Thursday morning Rick was sleeping peacefully. The night before, when they reached home, he'd collapsed across the foot of his bed. All the way home he'd been quiet. Mrs. C. had left him alone with his thoughts. She had looked in on him during the night. He was sleeping like a baby. He was perfectly relaxed — and his face! She couldn't get over the feeling that his facial expression had changed completely.

Coming home later that day, she was met by Rick who told her, "Mother, I've been praying all day!" She knew it had to be true. The change on his face was her assurance.

Her son continued: "I want to go early to the Anaheim Stadium tonight. Last night a counselor who said his name was Lazlo talked to me a long while. He told me to go home, read the Bible, and pray. I figured I've tried everything else, so I did as he suggested.

"Monday night when I went down on that field those three men told me God had something very special for me. It made me mad then, but today I've been thinking that if God really does want my life, He can have it, but if He's going to do something with me He'll have to show me in a definite way. Mother, I've given my life to God before and it's never worked; do you think this time it's real?"

Mother and son got into the car and headed east toward the Santa Ana Freeway. Once again Rick was wearing his grubbies.

"Mother, I've got it!" he exclaimed. "Just all of a sudden God has shown me that Christ is in my heart. I feel it! Look at me!"

Mrs. C. looked at her son and saw goose bumps up and down his arms. His face looked cleansed. Rick continued: "The only way I can explain it is that I feel like I was out on my bike and the wind is hitting my face and it feels just beautiful."

Answers started coming to Rick by the dozens, answers to questions he'd been asking himself for so long. They came as if somebody were telling them to him with words he could hear inside.

As they walked up to the stadium entrance, Rick was laughing. "I feel so good. I feel so good. I want to see every one of those counselors who've been talking to me all week."

Mrs. C. was concerned that he wouldn't find them all. Rick replied, "Don't worry, they're going to find me. . . ." That night every man who had attempted in some way to help Rick that week found him!

His step was light, not an affected jauntiness as before. Someone called out, "Rick!" He turned and saw one of the men who had counseled with him. He grabbed Rick's hand and said, "How do you feel, Rick?"

"I found Him!" Rick was almost shouting.

"Whom did you find?"

"You know . . ."

"Tell me; I want to hear you say it."

"I found Christ!" Rick felt like leaping into the air.

That was Rick's first witness. Later he was to remark, "That counselor was really wise. He didn't just let me get away with casually saying, 'I found Him,' but he made me tell him and I've been telling everybody since!"

That night Rick's mother once again sat apart from her son. She wondered, when the invitation was given, if Rick would go forward. But it wasn't necessary; his decision had been made. Rick sat still, happily watching. Later, when everyone was leaving, John came over to Rick. Soon Lionel and Lazlo joined them. Rick's mother had kept her eyes on the scene and she saw them all turn and look toward her. In a moment Rick was bringing them twenty rows up and introducing her. John suggested they all join for dinner the next night. It seemed like a good idea.

Friday night Mrs. C. hoped Rick would discard his grubbies. When she ventured the suggestion that he dress up, he replied, "No, they like me this way." She had hung out his favorite white sport coat; now she hung it away with his black pants. It took strength to hold back, but she did not force the issue. Something restrained her. Later Rick related his feelings to me about the grimy trousers.

"I liked my grubbies. God hadn't told me that I shouldn't wear them. But that night when we went out to dinner, as I was sitting there with all of them looking so nice, for the first time I felt bad that I'd worn those grubbies. That was when God gave me reason for never wearing them again."

At that point Rick jumped up and the next thing I knew he was holding in front of me the greasiest, dirtiest jeans I have ever seen — his grubbies! He also showed me his belt and bracelet, both made from a motorcycle chain, heavy and very dangerous looking. "I am going to burn my grubbies. I haven't had them on since that night. And neither have I been near my motorcycle. I have no desire to jump on my bike and take off anymore. Also, I haven't touched a cigarette since all of this happened to me, nor the drugs, and I don't intend to."

Friday night on the way out of the stadium, Rick and his mother were passing the television trailer when a man who had seen Rick the night he was surrounded at the speaker's platform came over to him. He held out his hand and Rick recognized the bikers' grip! Rick was impressed. At that moment Cliff Barrows came out of the trailer and the TV man introduced Rick to Cliff. Rick said, "I am the one that caused the disturbance on the field the other night." It was plain to Cliff Barrows that a transformation had taken place in this young man!

Saturday evening Rick came to the Crusade wearing black pants, white jacket, black tie, and a shirt with lace on the cuffs, a style that is popular with some of the fellows in southern California. After the service Rick walked down to the platform. He looked up at Cliff Barrows who, at that moment, happened to spot him. Cliff called him up on the platform. People all around were waiting for Cliff's autograph, but Cliff took Rick and introduced him to others on the platform and then, taking Rick aside, prayed with him.

If it was apparent to Cliff Barrows that Rick had changed, it was especially obvious to Lionel. He had been with Rick on the field that first Monday and had watched Rick closely all week. Lionel says, "It is the most dramatic conversion experience I have witnessed in twenty years of working with Billy Graham and Campus Crusade for Christ." The acid eyes had been cleansed.

7

Faces from the Crowd

Saturday night — a good night to take your girl to a drive-in movie. That's what 18-year-old Doug thought as he picked up Susie in Costa Mesa and slipped into the traffic on the Santa Ana Freeway.

The traffic was terrible, much worse than usual. Doug maneuvered his car skillfully but not skillfully enough. The next thing he knew they were in the midst of a stream of cars exiting at Katella and being swept toward the parking lot of Anaheim Stadium. "Well, this is a switch." Doug smiled wryly at Susie. "What do you suggest we do?"

"Let's go in and see what it's all about," she dared him. They did. And they came out later a little dazed by the sudden turnabout in their lives. Billy Graham, a famous evangelist but a stranger to them, had come across as no movie idol ever had. Jesus Christ, a religious leader of the past, had become their living Savior, they indicated on their decision cards.

A visiting high school football team from Santa Ana may have seen Graham somewhat as David Shaw, *Los Angeles Times* writer, did when he described the evangelist as beginning his sermon "with a Bible tucked, football-style, beneath his arm." The young gridders heard Billy thunder:

"The gods of America have failed the young people of this nation. . . . Our American gods will not bring young people the peace, the joy, the happiness that they are looking for. They are rebelling against the gods of sex, leisure, pleasure, entertainment, and materialism. They are saying, 'Give me a God to believe in, give me a faith to follow.' "

Eleven of the fifty-plus gridders shouldered their way to the platform after the service to invite Christ into their lives.

Thirteen-year-old Rex was something else. Spitting from the top balcony and zinging artfully folded Crusade programs out over the audience was great fun. He'd come to the Crusade with his neighbor, 13-year-old Bill. He really didn't want to come, but he was restless at home, so he went.

When the stadium was full and tarpaulins were being placed on the outfield grass for people to sit on, Rex said, "Hey, let's go down there instead." After the service Rex whispered to Bill, "Let's go closer and look at Billy Graham."

Bill, a Christian, replied, "We're not going forward unless you are willing to accept Christ as your Savior; I've already accepted Him."

Without any hesitation Rex said, "OK, I am; let's go."

Was it for real? In the presence of the counselor, the rough and tumble boy broke into tears. Later, on the way out of the stadium Rex said, "Now I'll have to find new friends. . . ."

Bill's father asked, "Did you enjoy the service, Rex?" A quiet, subdued Rex answered, "I accepted Christ as my Savior." The next morning, an hour and a half before Bill and his family were due to leave for Sunday school, Rex rang the doorbell to ask if he would go with them. And he kept on going.

Kitty, a waitress at a Mexican restaurant in nearby Orange, was going through the agonies of a second divorce while mothering two small children and working to support them. She went alone to the Crusade one night and left with Christ as her companion.

Kitty could hardly wait to get to the restaurant the next day. Her glow was obvious to everyone in the restaurant. "You must come with me to the Billy Graham Crusade at the Angels Stadium," she urged. And some came to see what had changed Kitty.

Her uncle and his two sons came the next night and made the discovery that it was a Person, Jesus Christ, who transforms a person's life. Like a stone dropped into a pond, the witness of Kitty and her uncle lapped at other lives.

On Wednesday Rosalie, 24-year-old cook at the restaurant, could no longer resist seeing for herself what was going on at the Crusade. Rosalie traces her ancestry to the Aztec Indians in Mexico. Her background in another faith did not prevent an openhearted acceptance of Jesus Christ.

That same evening Ramona, wife of the manager, accompanied Rosalie and Kitty, and she also reached out and received.

The Bible says that villagers streamed from Sychar to see Jesus at the village well where a woman's spiritual thirst was quenched. Kitty, the once-thirsty waitress, could understand that woman.

While there was much emphasis on youth at the Crusade and thousands of youth responded, entire families also came forward together.

A husband and wife who did not come to the Crusade together "found each other" after both "found Christ" on the Angels' field. The youthful counselor whose privilege it was to help them exclaimed later, "Man, that was really neat!"

A counselor talked to a man and his two sons, ages fourteen and twelve, then turned to counsel a lady nearby. The counselor ascertained her name and in surprise said, "I just checked off a man and two boys over there with the same name," and he pointed a short distance away. The lady turned and gasped, "My family!" and rushed to them. Her surprise and joy was so great she could not talk, but neither could her husband and sons. They were reconciled in Christ!

A middle-aged couple talking with a counselor was joined by a young man who said, "I would like to do this, too." The mother turned and said, "Now look, Dad and I are dead serious about this. Are you?" The son put his arms around his mother and said, "Yes, Mom, I am, I really am." The three bowed their hearts in a prayer of submission.

Southern California abounds with servicemen on leave or off duty for an evening, particularly in the area surrounding Disneyland and the Angel Stadium. They came to the Crusade by the hundreds. Records indicate that 188 of them came forward to make decisions. Of this number 117 were first-time commitments; the remainder were for rededication and assurance.

At least one, a corporal in the Marine Corps at El Toro, was counseled by one of his superior officers, Major Hitchcock, an advisor. Brigadier General Henry W. Hise, commandant of El Toro Marine Air Station, was military chairman on the Crusade executive committee. The general had recently returned from Vietnam where he had served as assistant commander of the First Marine Air Wing at Da Nang. His strong support of the Crusade made possible nightly visits by Marines and their families on buses which arrived early and stayed late. General Hise himself was a platform guest.

Perhaps one of the most touching of the Crusade stories concerned a 21-year-old seaman apprentice who was stationed aboard the U.S.S. *Okinawa* in drydock at Long Beach. He had come out of curiosity. After praying and giving his life to Christ, the seaman told his counselor, "This is something I've put off for too long. It's something I really want to do." The counselor then turned and introduced him to an advisor, who happened to be a Navy chaplain in civilian clothes. While he was talking to the advisor, another ship's chaplain came by, saw the sailor and stopped. Then it was discovered that the second chaplain was from the boy's ship! Two other sailors in civilian clothes came by and extended a welcome to the seaman to visit the Christian Fellowship Center in Long Beach. He was well launched!

Roger was a 19-year-old soldier in the Second Replacement Company Staging Battalion at Camp Pendleton. He came to Anaheim to visit Disneyland but found it closed for the evening. He remembered an advertisement in the paper about the Crusade at the stadium and headed there. That night he signed up for the Lord's army.

Roger, like all the inquirers, received a red booklet entitled *Knowing Christ*. It contained the Gospel of John, words of encouragement from Billy Graham, Bible-verse cards to memorize, and the first lesson of a Bible correspondence course to be completed and sent to the Graham office in Minneapolis.

The message of Billy Graham was "heard" by 652 people through their eyes — they were the deaf and hard of hearing. Nightly, at the stadium's left field line at press level, a section was reserved for this select group whose fervor was something to see. It was the Rev. Delbert L. Hosteller's responsibility to coordinate all of the arrangements. He was well qualified to do this as the pastor of the Immanuel Church of the Deaf in Los Angeles. Two counselors were on hand each night, rotating and interpreting everything from the preliminaries through the last "Amen." Of the fifteen counselors assigned to this section, ten were deaf. Thirty-five people from this group went forward during the Crusade, and ten of them were first-time decisions. Included was a deaf boy who had grown up on crutches. Dave swung his way through the masses of people on the field to a counselor and there invited Christ into his heart.

A Santa Barbara College student came forward and related to her counselor that she had accepted Christ in a "hearing" church; however, due to her deafness she had difficulty in comprehending and she drifted away. Conviction weighed heavily when she learned of the Crusade and she drove 125 miles to "hear" and respond.

A 60-year-old visitor, Mr. Barnes, was both deaf and blind. Could he "hear" without seeing the interpreter? Yes, he received the message from an interpreter beside him who pressed the message into the palm of the sightless man with his fingers. Mr. Barnes, sensing the variation of shapes, responded with great emotion and indicated his desire to rededicate his life to his Lord.

One Christian deaf youth drove all the way from Phoenix, Arizona, to "hear" the message of Billy Graham by sign language. The Bible says, "In that day shall the deaf hear the words of the book" (Isaiah 29:18). No one was excluded from hearing in Anaheim Stadium.

The impact of the Billy Graham Crusade was seen and felt on school and college campuses throughout southern California. A high school principal who had been antagonistic to Christianity brightened at the sight of the Team-designed mod book covers turning up on student's books. "This is what we need," he observed. A journalism instructor at the same school conceded: "You can say what you want to say about Christianity as long as you don't preach." The book covers said a lot without preaching!

Gordon, a medical student at Loma Linda, appreciated the good news his counselor shared with him so much that he wanted to pay for the service! When Gordon took out his wallet the counselor told him, "Just go back to school and show your appreciation for what Christ has done for you by living as a Christian."

Another student said, "Jesus Christ has been in my head; tonight He invaded my heart. I can hardly wait to 'get going' for God."

Ousha, a young Hindu doing graduate study in nuclear medicine at UCLA, went forward to make a decision. Just beginning her second year of study, Ousha came to the Crusade at the invitation of Dr. Delores Johnson, director of the UCLA department of Nuclear Medicine at Harvard General Hospital in Torrance. At the end of the service Ousha stood to go forward. Dr. Johnson, a counselor, went forward to counsel an older woman, but was happily diverted when she saw Ousha standing next to her. "I had the joy of counseling my dear Ousha," she said later.

Many from cult groups came to recognize their error of following false doctrines. Susan, whose husband deserted her and their three children four years previously, came from the San Fernando Valley. She told her counselor, "I want to get back to reading the Bible instead of the religious book I have been studying."

Dan Endresen, 21-year-old counselor, talked to a 40-year-old gentleman from a cult who called himself a chronic procrastinator, believing what was in the Bible but never ready to accept God's terms. Now he wanted to do what Christ told him in the Bible.

Billy's brother Melvin, forty-three, a dairy farmer from Charlotte, North Carolina, came to this Crusade and sat on the platform with his world-famous brother. When Billy introduced him, Melvin said simply, "Thank you, preacher." The audience responded with welcoming applause. Billy had said, "God called me to preach, and Melvin to stay at home and farm. . . . There is no man I love and respect more than my brother." It was a touching tribute.

Melvin Graham, comparing himself to what Moses once said of himself, stated, "I too have been slow in mind, slow in tongue and have had no real talent like Billy . . . but God has shown me that He will direct our lives when we are willing to allow Him to do this very thing. . . ." His testimony was brief, but it was used by God.

In one case, a minister who had been trusting in his baptism and good works for salvation saw, through Melvin, that he was going the wrong way, and he turned around spiritually.

On the same night a man in front of the platform yelled out, "I'm an alcoholic from Alaska — is there any hope for me?" A hush fell over the vast crowd as Billy quietly, compassionately assured him, "Yes, there is hope for you. . . ." And then addressing himself to all, he said, "Tonight I've been talking to you about the blood — Christ's blood. Jesus' blood covers all sins. It is as though you had never sinned at all. . . ."

An interested worker in the stadium follow-up office tabulated the vocations of many of the inquirers. She discovered that eighty-four entertainers had accepted second billing behind Christ, fifty-eight policemen and security guards asked soul protection, forty-seven news and feature writers began a new story, and thirty-nine people in the housing industry secured down payments on their heavenly mansions. Among vocations not strongly represented, according to the incomplete survey, were those in scientific fields. Nine pharmacists made decisions, but a lone "scientist" was found by the tabulator to have examined the evidence and seen the answer in Christ. Six opticians, however, recognized Jesus as their Lord.

Evangelists have always said salvation cleans up a person. The owner of a Santa Ana laundry put it this way: "This is the off-season for the shirt-laundry business. But our business has suddenly gone beyond any volume we've ever had for this time of year. I've called all the laundries in the area, and they all say the same. The only thing we can figure out is that hundreds of additional people are attending the Billy Graham Crusade wearing clean shirts!"

Billy, recalling the faces of youth captured by *Life* magazine photographers at the Woodstock rock music festival, commented, "They left with the same sad and lonely faces. They were looking for something and they did not find it. The young people who responded here have found what they're looking for. There is joy and peace in their faces."

Whether they were swept into the "Big A" on a tidal wave of traffic, impelled by curiosity or boredom, or driven by an urgent sense of need, thousands of faces came alive at the stadium and began to reflect the glory of the Savior they had met.

8

High Adventure

Counselor "Teddy" McMichael felt one evening during the Crusade that she was working her guardian angel overtime. As she left her seat high in the stadium and stepped down on the playing field to counsel, she realized that she had left her purse behind in the stands. Her dilemma hit her with a thud as she observed scores of people in her immediate area who needed counseling. At that moment an advisor called out, "Lady counselors needed back at home plate. . . ." That's where she was. How could she possibly go back after her purse?

Teddy looked around and saw the two girls the advisor had motioned her to follow. She could see that they definitely needed help. Quickly she prayed: "Lord, You take care of my purse; I'll take care of these two girls for You." She approached the girls, began talking to them earnestly, and moments later had the joy of seeing them make decisions for Christ.

Afterward Teddy made her way back up into the stadium. When she reached the area where she had been sitting she saw a man standing near her seat. When she reached down to retrieve her purse he said with a smile: "I've been guarding it. It hasn't been touched!"

There were hundreds of others who believed guardian angels were working overtime as stories from the counselors and advisors began to surface. The unusual experiences, the seeming coincidences, the kind of folk who were making decisions, all combined to make it easy to believe in miracles.

Who were these counselors and advisors? They came from all walks of life: professional men and women, servicemen, housewives, college and high school students, laborers, factory workers, ministers — all interested in and eager to help those who would respond and come forward at the Crusade. They are vital to the success of any Crusade. Not just casual volunteers called in for one night's duty, they are the product of a concentrated effort involving once-a-week training for five weeks. These Christian Life and Witness Classes saw eight thousand people attending instruction which was taught by various Team members in churches throughout the southern California area.

The Rev. Harry Williams, Crusade director, said, "These classes made a major contribution to the training of the laity for the continuing task of evangelism through the local church. They are designed to give practical instruction in living a Christian life in today's society and helping the lay members of the church understand something of the principles, importance, values, and methods of sharing their faith. Each person who responded to Mr. Graham's invitation to come forward at the close of the meeting was paired with one of these trained counselors. The counselor talked individually with the person. Also, the counselors had the responsibility to befriend those they counseled and to encourage them to become involved in a local church."

Assisting in the teaching were Henry Holley and Don Tabb of the Team. These men were all experienced, having conducted similar classes in various parts of the world. Materials for their classes were provided by the Graham Association. To qualify as a counselor, individuals had to attend three out of five sessions. Standards were high, but for good reason, as was to be seen in some of the difficult counseling situations which these people were to encounter.

Advisors for the most part were church pastors or youth pastors and other specially trained and qualified individuals. When a counselor encountered a difficult situation, he could turn to an advisor, who was easily identified by a special badge with ribbon, and the advisor would take over. Advisors came to Gate 6 each night to pick up their assignments and leave with a group of counselors for a reserved area in the stadium. When the service was concluded the advisor would stand and motion to his counselors, one by one, pairing them with inquirers by age and sex as much as possible. It was an effective way of dealing with the thousands who were coming forward. Many of the counselors and advisors were themselves converts of Billy's earlier Los Angeles Crusades. Hampton and Sue Riley were typical of such.

Sue, soft-spoken, blonde wife of a leading layman in Orange County, came over to me one evening on the field. "I'm so excited," she said. "I counseled this couple — he came down to accept Christ for the first time, and she rededicated her life. It was so real! I shared with them what happened to Hampton and me twenty years ago, on the 16th of September at Billy's Los Angeles Crusade! Hampton didn't have a Christian background and came forward then, and I rededicated my life — just like this couple. . . ." Her face was radiant.

Hamp Riley had many interesting counseling experiences. One evening he saw a well-dressed Negro couple slide into their stadium seats with an air of eager anticipation. When the invitation to come forward was given, he noticed they were out of their seats immediately and were one of the first couples down on the field. Riley followed in the line of duty.

As he counseled with them, the man revealed: "I told my wife, 'I want to be saved. How do you get saved?' She said, 'I don't know, but I hear Billy Graham is going to be in southern California. Let's hop on a flight and find out.' So here we are." Beside him his wife chimed in, "We found out!" This couple had come on a late afternoon flight from San Francisco just in time to attend the evening meeting.

Joan Denemy, a red-haired designer living in Anaheim, had gone to the 1963 Crusade in Los Angeles' Memorial Coliseum. Joan would understand and be able to identify with those she would counsel. She had been, in her own words, "very deep in the world, mixing with the wrong people, and my life was crumbling. I had a desperate need, a hunger. I had no peace, a complete vacuum. When I heard the Gospel, I was sold. It was so beautiful. Billy introduced me to Christ . . ." Another counselor reported that of thirty-seven persons she had counseled in the Los Angeles Crusade six years before, eighteen were still corresponding with her.

Fashion model Jan arrived breathless at Gate 6 each evening for her counseling assignment. Looking every bit a representative of her profession, she would share her counseling experiences of the evening before. "I feel as if I have a blind date every night," she exclaimed. "One night," Jan continued, "I saw an attractively dressed girl coming in. She sat not too far from me. I started praying for her as I've never prayed for anyone before. When Billy gave the invitation, sure enough, she went forward. She was so composed. And then, oh, it was wonderful, my advisor motioned to me to follow her. I stayed right behind her, thinking, praying, wondering. And then I stepped slightly to the side, and saw tears coming down her cheeks. I thought: O dear Lord, help me to say the right things. . . ." She was able to see the girl give herself without reservation to Christ in a first-time decision. In Jan's words: "We were able to communicate so beautifully and I went home walking on air. And I'll be able to follow-up with her because she, too, is a model and we'll be in many fashion shows together."

Foreign language counselors, forty-seven strong, turned out to do a special work nightly. They counseled in Portuguese, Czechoslovakian, German, Hungarian, Rumanian, Russian, Swedish, French, Spanish, Chinese, Japanese, Yiddish, and Dutch. A Los Angeles housewife of Jewish background accepted Christ as her Savior with great sobs, but would not give her name, saying. "My husband will persecute me if he finds out." A 53-year-old minister from a Dutch-background church sought assurance along with his wife, the latter saying she had really asked Christ into her life for the first time. A Redondo Beach high school exchange student from the Netherlands came with an American girl friend. She told her Dutch counselor, "My eyes have been opened. I didn't know I had to accept Christ like that to be a Christian."

A lady who spoke German fluently occupied a seat that had been reserved by another counselor for a non-Christian friend. She was politely requested to find another seat. Later the lady searched until she found the counselor to explain how "all things work together for good," quoting from Romans 8:28. "I want you to know," she said, "that you were supposed to have me move. I went and sat elsewhere, and of all the people in that huge stadium that I should choose to sit behind, the couple ahead of me was speaking German. When Billy gave the invitation they went forward. I decided to follow. I know God put me there because I was able to communicate in German to them."

One excited counselor reported: "I talked to a boy and his dad who is the principal of an area high school. The boy accepted Christ and I phoned him the next night. I asked what he'd been doing, and whether he'd been telling others. His answer really thrilled me. He said, 'I'm going to give a speech on what happened to me at the Billy Graham Crusade in my speech class tomorrow.' "

Dave, Maury, and Lee were counselors whose own lives would make stories. Dave's khaki-colored jacket, with its hood pulled up tight over his head and tied under his chin, his grubby looking corduroys and bare feet in heavy brown sandals made him easy to spot every night. He and his friends were no joke, though they looked it.

Lee's mother sat at a table near the entrance for counselors, handing out badges and assisting as she could. She showed me a "before" picture of her son. Could this be the same young man? "We went forward as a family at the 1963 Los Angeles Crusade," she said. "Lee was thirteen then. His commitment was real and it's lasted. Just think, at this Crusade he's a counselor!"

Dave, Maury, and Lee mingled nightly with the inquirers on the turf, opening their Bibles, grasping a hippyish-looking fellow by the arm, shaking someone's hand and bowing their heads in prayer after earnestly talking with them. Spectators who may have wondered at first about these odd-looking counselors had some of their faith restored in today's youth.

Billy Graham said on the first Saturday Youth Night: "I think there has been a change in the attitude of young people today, and I like what I see." Perhaps he was referring partly to attitudes displayed by some of these young counselors — compassion, courage, and involvement.

As Billy went to bat for America's young people, one could sense the warmth he was generating among them. "It is the older generation," he accused, "that sells the drugs, makes the lewd films, and sets the critical tone for our age."

Aiming straight at parents he lashed out, "If you don't train your child before he is ten, you may have lost him. . . . Young people want parents to be patient, to listen to them and to set examples of integrity and truthfulness."

In the audience was a group of kids from Joplin's Boy's Ranch, a rehabilitation center for delinquent youths — youths who were the victims of what Billy Graham had described. Counselors Lee, Maury, and Dave sat behind the kids and later moved quickly into action when the fellows from the Boy's Ranch responded to Billy's challenge to commit their lives to Christ.

Drugs — or nothing else — gave a thrill like this, the counselors agreed.

9

Front Page Story

In the fall of 1949, when Evangelist Billy Graham and his Team members wore wide, hand-painted ties with jackets, trousers, and shirts to match, the *Los Angeles Times* commented that he "appeared to be a rainbow gone berserk." Twenty years later *Times* staff writer David Shaw referred to him as a "subtler Billy Graham but still crackling thunder." But, Shaw added, "There is little else subtle or conventional or middle-aged about Graham with a sermon in his hand and a crowd in his grasp. The tall, athletic body is still lean and hard, the blue eyes still flash the fire of righteous indignation, the voice still cracks the sound of impending doom. Graham is a robust, vigorous, 6-foot 2½-inch, 170-pounder, and as he stands atop the platform over second base in Anaheim Stadium during his 10-day Southern California Crusade, he seems the embodiment, the quintessence, of all that is good and strong and vital in man." Such a description of a 50-year-old Christian contrasts curiously with the recent remark of matinee and TV idol Tom Jones: "I hate to think of being fifty when I can't do anything I want."

Reporters delighted in keeping the public informed about the Graham attire. The Anaheim *News Bulletin* said, "He looked youthful last night in an electric blue sports coat and black slacks. . . ." And indeed, Billy Graham did look sharp and healthy. Clothier Earl Mooney, a close friend, took particular pride in seeing that Billy dressed well and comfortably.

The journalists on the scene did their best to come up with new ways of describing Billy in action. Bob Norek, Fullerton *Daily News Tribune* suburban editor, did an exceptional job reporting every phase of the Crusade. "His whole being is in motion as he presents his message," he wrote. "He draws geometric patterns in the air, then wipes them clean with one sweep of his hands. His hands jab as if he were slicing fresh bread. At times he carried the Bible around the platform as if he were O. J. Simpson lugging the pigskin to score six." Bob Ziebell, another Fullerton editor, noted, "Dr. Graham tells it like it is. The source he quotes from — the Bible — has the deepest roots of all, and the message it offers is clear and unchanged."

It was this unchanging message of Christ that changed the destinies for thousands of people who made decisions. The newspaper coverage had considerable to do with getting them there. Mr. Graham recognized the fact, as did Team members and others who were concerned and praying about the meetings.

From the platform Billy mentioned several times the outstanding work done by local reporters, photographers, and editors. Later these individuals, as well as publishers, were to receive personal letters from Dr. Graham thanking them for their superb work. One such letter said, ". . . I know how difficult a religious event can be to interpret to the general readership of a daily newspaper. I feel that you did a very professional job and I am indebted to you for extending the outreach of the Crusade. . . ."

Bob Norek's written appraisal so often seemed to convey the heart of what Billy Graham was preaching. I asked Norek for a personal reaction to what he was seeing. "The Crusade was impressive, an event that everyone should take in when it comes their way. Billy Graham preaches Jesus Christ and God the Father. There is no parochialism in his messages. They are basic Christianity. He reminds me of one of the old Bible prophets — except he has forsaken rough cloaks for smart-looking sport coats — 'crying in the wilderness' of these times. I was particularly impressed by the 'decision' segment of this Crusade."

Another newspaper which provided blanket coverage of the event was the *Santa Ana Register*. Clay Miller, photographer, told me, "During the ten days Billy was here, nothing happened that pushed him off page one — no fires, no world events, no kidnapings, no holdups, not even the earthquake in northern California. Billy Graham was number one news. There were pictures and stories every day. One day we actually felt we had printed too much about the Team and the Crusade. There were four stories, one about the Crusade meeting, one about the deaf spectators, one about Mrs. Pearl Goode (Billy's prayer warrior), and one about Ruth Graham's recipes for Chinese food!"

Paul Travis, Santa Ana columnist who writes a folksy column, "Front Porch Chats," published an interview with Billy Graham in which he reported, "It was perhaps the most famous chat I've ever had. . . ." Incidentally, Miller and Travis met every Thursday morning for prayer for over a year while the Crusade was in preparation, and then during the Crusade. They asked the Lord to bring to southern California the full impact of what the Graham Team stands for, and to show how Christ could change lives.

Mary Ann Leuenberger, photographer-reporter from the Anaheim *Bulletin*, was another enthusiastic observer. Nightly she was in the press box or on the field taking pictures and picking up exciting stories. She declared that this Crusade was the most newsworthy event she had covered in twenty years on the paper; and her stories reflected it.

Other newspapers up and down the southern coast, from Santa Barbara to San Diego, kept the Crusade in the forefront of people's thinking by coverage that was termed unprecedented — and effective!

They came, they saw—Jesus conquered. Area Crusade director Harry Williams and Billy survey the waiting stadium.

Overflow audience spills across the outfield as thousands tune in to the Gospel.

A packed stadium, typical of countless opportunities for God in today's troubled world.

Soul-set-free: the Kinsfolk with something to sing about.

Behind the scenes—where hundreds work to follow up conversions with personal counseling and correspondence courses.

The "tomorrow generation" gets in on the action at a Crusade.

Bearded counselor helps an inquirer find the answers in the Scripture.

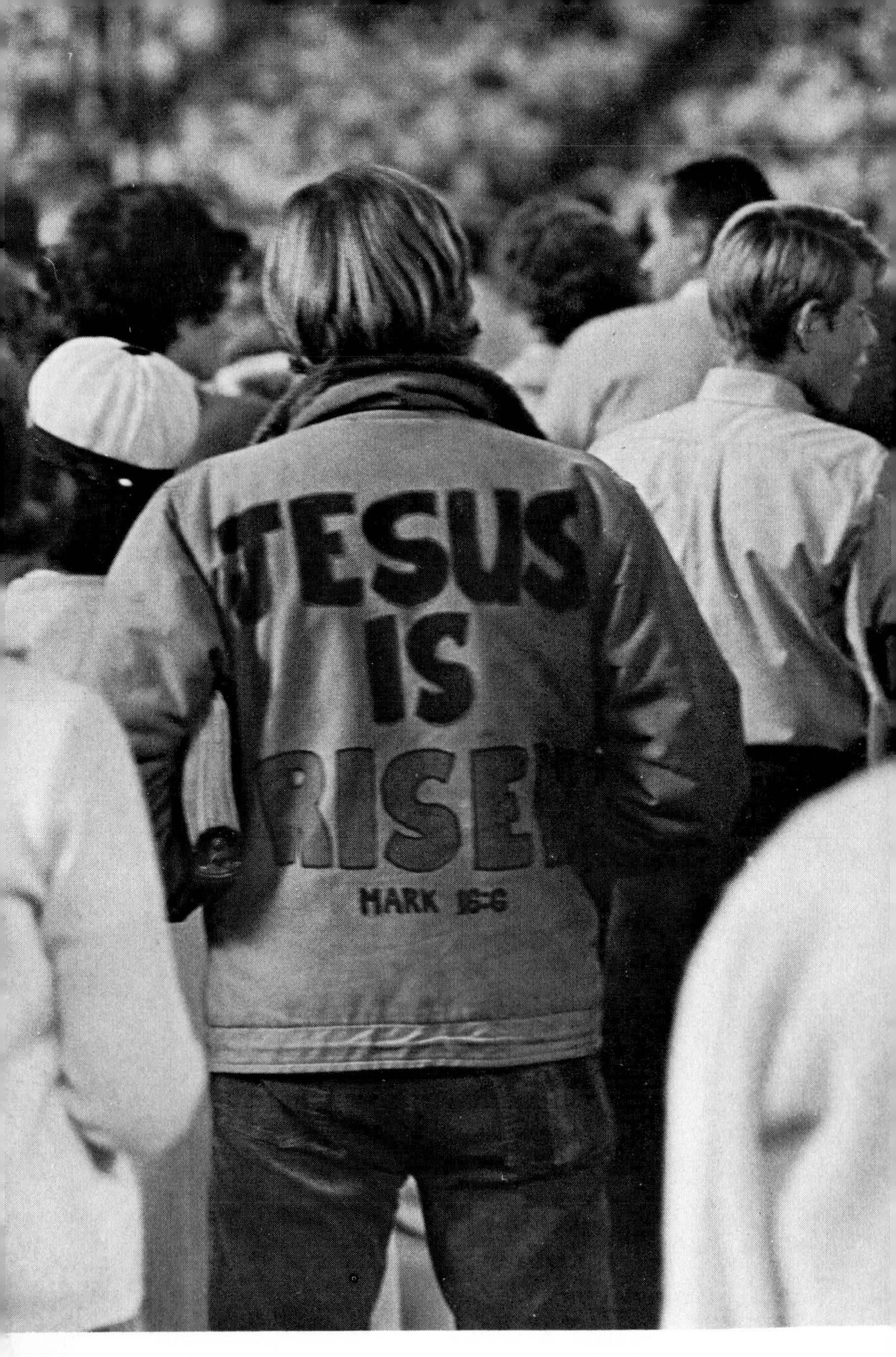

Crusades come to an end, but the Word is the future's hope.

10

A Day with Billy

When Billy Graham walks to the podium to speak at an evening Crusade meeting, he looks so rested, relaxed, and impeccably groomed that it would be easy to assume he has spent the day in bed. Nothing could be further from the truth. Every day of the Anaheim Crusade was filled with activity, as though Judgment Day were next!

Nobody knows where Billy inherited his boundless energy and enthusiasm. It might have been from his farmer father who was forced to work sixteen hours a day to make a living for his family of six. Or it could have been from his Scottish mother whose progenitors were known for their stamina. Or it could be a special gift from God to enable him to cope with his superhuman schedule and responsibilities. At any rate, he is one of the most active and tireless men in the world. One of his Team members said: "Keeping up with Billy is like keeping pace with a bulldozer. He can think of more things to do and get more people doing them than any man I ever heard of."

But Billy is not just an idea man. He takes the lead in getting the job done. If an average person were to follow him through one day's appointments and duties, he would drop from sheer exhaustion.

Let's take an average day in the life of Billy Graham. The days of the Anaheim Crusade were typical, one of which went like this.

After having retired at midnight, Graham bounced out of bed at 6 A.M. and began his morning routine. First he shaved his heavy, blond beard — so heavy he'd have to shave again about 5 P.M. Next he showered. Then he dampened his thick, unruly mop of hair, combed it, and pressed a golf cap over it to hold it in place. He walked to the night stand, picked up his well-worn, marked Bible, and turned to the book of Psalms. He says the Psalms teach him about our relationship to God, and the Proverbs of his relationship to men. He usually reads five Psalms and one chapter of Proverbs a day.

After Bible reading and prayer, he dictated his sermon notes for the evening. Sometimes when he has an early morning appointment, he dictates his sermon notes the night before. He rarely uses old sermon material, preferring to freshen up his messages with up-to-date quotes and illustrations.

At 7 A.M. T. W. Wilson, his executive secretary, joined Billy for breakfast and briefed him regarding appointments for the day. First on the agenda was a series of conferences with his associates. On his staff are ten evangelists who conduct Crusades on every continent. Billy is responsible for the guidance and financing of these missionary undertakings. His annual budget for all arms of his ministry is $15,000,000, and he relies upon freewill offerings and contributions for this tremendous budget. It is a faith ministry in every sense of the word.

In 1966 Graham co-sponsored the World Congress of Evangelism in Berlin. He himself conducts one or more Crusades abroad each year. In 1969 he campaigned in Australia and Austria. These Crusades require hours of collaboration and planning, and hundreds of people to implement the plans. Graham is involved in every substantial decision and must make a personal determination on major issues. A constant stream of associates and colleagues beat a path to his door wherever he is and no matter how busy he is.

At 11:30 Billy left the Newport Inn for a luncheon with Anaheim Mayor Lorin Griset and other members of the Crusade executive committee. There Billy greeted each man by name and visited leisurely with them, as though he had nothing else to do. Somehow he manages to treat each individual as if he were the most important person in the world.

As the meal was served and items of business were discussed, Dr. Graham showed no signs of hurry. Then T. W. Wilson reminded him it was time to leave if they were to make their appointment with Gene Autrey, owner of the Anaheim Angels baseball team. Billy is at home with celebrities and "names" in world politics. He has met hundreds of world leaders and thousands of well-known personalities. With all, he shares his easy-going manner and skips from light banter to serious conversation.

One appointment that stimulated Billy greatly was with Golda Meir, Prime Minister of Israel. Mrs. Meir could not have been more affable and Billy could not have enjoyed an interview more. After all, the One whom he serves was a Jew, and he well realizes the important part Israel plays in the divine drama of the ages.

Billy opened the conversation by saying: "Madame Prime Minister, did you know that my daughter and her husband have had a home in Israel for the past three years?" Mrs. Meir replied that she had heard that "Gigi" often visited Israel, but she was not aware they lived there. They chatted informally about some of the problems of the Middle East and parted with the customary Israeli farewell, "Shalom."

One visit Billy considered very important was with Kaleen Ladd, the Crusade director's secretary, who was injured in a tragic car accident the first Sunday of the Crusade. Enroute to the stadium, the car in which she was riding with her husband collided with another and Kaleen suffered serious brain damage. The doctors attending her held no hope of recovery, but many prayers were offered for her. Billy drove over the packed freeways to visit Kaleen, her husband, and her parents. With the family by the bedside, Billy took her limp hand and prayed compassionately for this young wife whose dedication to Christ had been an inspiration to all who knew her. She remained in a coma for several weeks, but as this book went to press she was showing some signs of recovery. When told of the success of the Anaheim Crusade, Kaleen said: "Oh, thank God."

After a flurry of afternoon appointments, Billy rang T. W.'s room and said, "I'm tired of talking. Let's play nine holes of golf on the pitch and putt course." In minutes they were on the green fairways of the par-three course of the Newport Inn. Billy plays golf not only for the exercise but also because it is one of the few things he can do in solitude. Almost everyone, especially golfers, will respect a man's privacy when he is on the "sacred turf."

From 5:30 to 6:30 is Graham's time to be alone. During the Crusades it is a law almost as binding as that of the Medes and Persians that no one interrupt him during that hour. He ordered a bowl of soup and a sandwich, then, lying on the bed, he studied his sermon notes for the evening and had a time of prayer.

At 6:30 Wilson arrived, and they started the 25-mile drive to Anaheim Stadium. There they entered the elevator and ascended to the third floor where a TV makeup man, producers, and several others were waiting in his private room. His brother, Melvin, a special Crusade guest, was there just to say "hello." His daughter Bunny kissed him on the cheek and said, "I haven't seen you for four days." Then the makeup man combed his hair and patted makeup on his face to soften the glare of the TV lights. All the services of the Anaheim Crusade were to be aired locally and three nationally, with an expected audience of about 20 million.

At 7:20 the platform group emerged from the Los Angeles Angels' dugout and walked across the infield. Billy shook hands with the executive committee members and then greeted each one in the guest section.

The demands of holding the attention of a large audience, keeping on cue for a TV tape and pouring compassion into an invitation to decide for Christ is almost a superhuman task. When the two-hour service is over, Billy has expended more energy than a farmer pitching hay for ten hours, say physicians.

After the service, a small group of Team members, police, and friends followed Billy to his car. Autograph fans were waiting for a coveted signature, and he obliged two or three of them quickly. As he saw the disappointment of others, he said: "Sorry, I haven't time for more." If he didn't get out before the crowd is dismissed, Billy would be mobbed by people who want to shake his hand. Billy, T. W. Wilson, Walter Smyth, and a president of a seminary in the Los Angeles area climbed into the car. Billy, disturbed as usual by people who hold him in awe, commented, "I wish people would think more of God and less of me. Sometimes I think I have failed by drawing attention to myself instead of to the Person of Christ."

But the day wasn't over. Billy had dinner with the seminary president, talked to Smyth about plans for the weekend, and conferred with T. W. about several overseas phone calls.

When he returned to his room, he picked up the phone and called his wife Ruth in Montreat, North Carolina. Later he reached for his Bible on the night stand and found the place in Proverbs where he had left off the night before. There was the verse his mother had taught him as a child: "In all thy ways acknowledge him, and he shall direct thy paths." This is one of the key verses in Billy's life, one to live by and to go to sleep by at the end of a full day.

11

An Experience

Doubtless some Californians regarded the doings at Anaheim Stadium as a bizarre "happening." It was big. It was unpredictable. It drew esoteric hippies. And things happened. But the events suggested age-old reality rather than novelty to observers, design rather than accident, as if they had not just happened. Many young people who had been on drugs had never been at a happening like this.

Just a week before the Crusade, Billy Graham had told a thousand ministers at the Anaheim Convention Center that the younger generation has a "hang-up" about the organized church and is searching in drugs and permissiveness for something it cannot find. "They use LSD as a substitute for the conversion we should have been preaching all the time. They want an experience; I've seen their haunting, wistful looks." Subsequent confessions by many inquirers at the Crusade corroborated Billy's view.

A 15-year-old girl said, "You just don't know the life I've lived up until tonight. But things will be different now. I want all my friends to know this man Jesus who I'm going to run around with now. He really loves kids like me, and He's taken away all my hurt. I didn't realize until tonight that someone could really love me like this."

Another girl, fourteen, admitted being on drugs. When the counselor talked to her she said, "I'm so relieved that you haven't asked me to confess everything to you." The counselor said, "If you tell the Lord, that's all that's necessary." She covered her face with her hands and cried unrestrained tears of joy and relief. Her prayer that followed was from a penitent heart yielded to Christ.

Greg, a former drug addict, revealed: "About seven months ago a friend invited me to join him in Bible study. I ridiculed the idea, but finally went out of curiosity. Before this I'd been on drugs twenty-four hours a day — you name it, I took it. That night I saw that Christ was the way, the truth and the life. Now I'm here at the Crusade, and look over there." He pointed to three boys being counseled. "Those are my old friends, and I'm going to bring others every night."

Fellows and girls such as this were finding their freeway trip to the Angel Stadium to be the end of a search, fellows like Frank who had been searching ever since he was sixteen. His early quest led him to take marijuana, LSD and "Speed" (Methedrine). When he told his family he was on drugs, they ordered him to leave home. Booted out of school, he got a job as a carpet layer. Supporting his habit was expensive and he found himself living on and from the streets. He sampled the San Francisco Haight-Ashbury hippie district before going into the Army.

Refusal to go to Vietnam, compounded by the fact that the military discovered narcotics in his possession, resulted in an undesirable discharge. And then July 20 came along. It was the date the astronauts first landed on the moon — and the date Frank almost died.

While he and a drunken friend were driving through Carbon Canyon on a winding stretch of road, a collision catapulted Frank from the rear seat and crushed his back. For two weeks Frank lay unconscious in a hospital. When he came to, he looked at himself and then looked around for a way to end it all. He was as good as dead, anyway.

Emory, a friend of Frank's, and his girl friend Nancy, visited Frank regularly. Christians themselves, they began giving Frank Gospel tracts and showing him Bible verses. Frank looked forward to seeing them, but when they invited him to attend the Billy Graham Crusade he was skeptical. "We'll get a wheelchair for you," they promised.

The first night of the Crusade Emory wheeled his friend up the stadium ramp — as he and Nancy prayed!

Billy Graham was saying, "Youth is crying out for a cause . . ." and Frank's attention was arrested. Curiosity had sent him on the drug kick — looking for an experience, yes, crying out for a cause. Yet that experience ended in a nightmare that wouldn't leave him even in blazing daylight.

When counselor Carl Zimmerman wheeled his own wheelchair alongside Frank's, the young man looked at him in surprise. He hadn't expected to find wheelchair companionship! Soon Carl was talking earnestly about the reality of Christ's second coming, just as Billy had preached, and the need for everyone to make a personal decision. Frank made his own decision for Christ that night.

Zimmerman visited Frank in the hospital frequently, amazing Frank and others with his wheelchair dexterity. Frank says there is only a slim chance he will ever walk again, but he is hopeful of getting to college and studying art. The formerly blank future looks promising. "If I had those years to live over again," Frank asserts, "I wouldn't touch drugs. I was curious, looking for an experience, but now I've had a *real* experience — I've found that Christ is the answer to my search."

Wes Roberts, youth pastor at a Whittier church, helped to assign counselors to advisors each evening. Afterward he got to meet some of the inquirers. Roberts had special reason to remember Billy's words one night.

"This is the crossroads of your life," warned the evangelist. "You must decide whether to continue down the road into deeper sin or to go upward by accepting God's offer of everlasting life. Remember the Bible tells us that without the shedding of blood there is no forgiveness. You need atonement. That can only be done through the blood. It is Adam's blood that flows through your veins and causes you the trouble. . . . You can be justified before God by accepting Jesus Christ as your Savior."

People moved past Roberts toward the platform after the service. Roberts spotted a young fellow with a high, wavy pompadour, dressed in tight jeans and black motorcycle boots, making his way through the crowd. A teenage counselor began talking with him as Roberts watched. Shortly the counselor, his face pale, came over to Roberts, followed by the biker. Wes gazed into the face of a clean-shaven, determined young man he guessed to be about nineteen. The counselor extended the information card to Roberts and he read: "John 'Mad Dog,' East Los Angeles War Lords."

Roberts extended his hand, introduced himself, and the young man said, "That Graham cat's no phony. He's for real. He's telling it just like I've wanted to hear it all my life. Yeah! For the first time I see God is real. . . ."

They talked earnestly. John "Mad Dog" made his decision there. "What will this do to your standing in your gang, John? Is this going to be a real decision?"

"You bet it is! Once we make a decision on something we never go back on it. My gang dared me to go forward; and now that I have, they won't dare say anything."

Roberts discovered that the War Lords are a teen version of Hell's Angels. He established a follow-up plan with John, and his church stands ready to welcome John and his friends. With help, John would go upward and onward with Christ, as Billy Graham had said.

"Buzz" Brase, truck driver for a bread company, counseled with two brothers, Stan, twenty, and Larry, eighteen. Stan wore very old clothes, had long, unkempt hair, and cried out, "Last night I O.D.'d (overdosed) on heroin again. I've got a vulture in my veins, a monkey on my back . . . My brother here found me; if it hadn't been for him I'd be dead tonight. Can God help me?" God had prepared Brase for this counseling experience and he was able to help Stan. Since then he has written numerous times to Stan and put him in touch with Christian agencies.

Julie, mother of a 17-year-old son, came to the Crusade

at the invitation of a friend. When Julie got separated from her friend, she felt panicky. Little wonder — she was living on tranquilizers by the mouthful. There were no empty seats where she was standing and she turned to leave, but a small, inner voice compelled her to stay. Rather than leave her position, she stood all through the service, smoking and drinking coffee from a large thermos she'd brought. When Billy invited decisions, she went forward hesitatingly, weeping.

Counselor Janet Lawhead followed Julie down. As they talked, Janet realized Julie was in desperate need. Her hands trembled so violently she had difficulty lighting and holding a cigarette. But Julie prayed to receive Christ. Janet debated about putting her through the added stress of meeting an advisor, which is a Crusade rule. She began to pray silently that God would send the right advisor along.

Advisor John Kimber appeared shortly, and Janet signaled to him. He came and was introduced to Julie. Suddenly Julie asked, "Mr. Kimber, did you teach school in Montebello?" Greatly surprised, he answered, "Yes, junior high. I was choral teacher."

Julie's recognition of Mr. Kimber relaxed her to the point where she poured out her heart to him. She had greatly admired him as a teacher, and now she knew she could speak to him of her great need. Janet mentioned how moments before she had asked God to send just the right advisor, and Julie said, "Do you mean God cared that much about me?"

Janet had Julie come to her home the next day. Because of immense problems in her life, Julie had developed complete dependence on tranquilizers. In March 1969 she had tried suicide. Then she resorted to more drugs — drugs to relax, drugs to get up, drugs to keep from thinking, drugs to keep going.

At Julie's first appointment with her psychiatrist following the Crusade, she told him, "After all this time I have been converted." His answer was, "What does it mean to be converted?" She replied, "I have accepted Christ as my Savior, and now I am calm and sure of myself because I have His strength to help me." The psychiatrist answered, "God is good, Christianity is wonderful, but sometimes God needs help." To this she said, "I have been so lonely; now I have a Friend who is always with me. He will help me."

A short time after the Crusade, Julie was able to shake her dependence on drugs for the first time in three years. She was able to return to work full time. The Bible is a living Book and her walk with the Lord a very real experience. Her pastor said to her, "Now you have more to live for than ever before because you have Christ and a compelling desire to help others." Julie told her counselor she wants to visit mental hospitals to tell what Christ has done for her. She still has problems, but now she has a Problem Bearer. "When things get rough, I remember Christ died for me — He loved me that much."

God's love was an experience that made all the others pale.

12

Sirens and Salvation

The importance of literature as an outreach of the Gospel of Jesus Christ was graphically demonstrated at the Anaheim Crusade. The story came from Millie Dienert, wife of Fred Dienert who, along with Walter Bennett, arranges the television coverage and "Hour of Decision" programs for the Billy Graham Evangelistic Association. Millie is a dynamic little woman who participates in many pre-crusade appearances for the Team. Such participation often takes her around the world, and the southern California Crusade saw her criss-crossing every freeway in the southland with the expertise of a native who is accustomed to the vast network of interchanges.

It seems a lady in Pomona had been reading Billy Graham's biography, written by John Pollock, and noticed the name "Elsner." She recognized it as belonging to Millie's father. She and Millie had been friends forty years earlier in Philadelphia. Further reading revealed that Millie had married Fred Dienert. "I remembered (she said later) seeing that name on the Billy Graham telecasts. Actually my one link with the Lord in all of these years was the 'Hour of Decision.' " She and her husband went on a vacation, and for the first time she shared with him what Christ had meant at one time in her life. Her husband's reply was, "If God wants you to find Millie Dienert, you'll find her." The wife said, "I believe He has already started!"

They came home from the vacation and looked at the stack of collected newspapers. The top newspaper carried the announcement that Mrs. Fred Dienert was speaking at Pomona Christian Women's Club.

This childhood friend called the astonished Millie on the phone and arranged to meet her at the luncheon. Afterward she invited Millie to her home, and Millie saw two hearts step into fellowship with the Lord. For the first time in all their years of marriage, prayer was offered at the family table.

Millie's comment after this dramatic encounter was, "Now I can pack my bags and go home. . . ." But of course she did not go home! She continued her busy round of appointments.

In Yorba Linda a couple were living far from God. The mother of the husband was praying for her daughter-in-law, wondering if she could convince her to accompany her to a brunch where Millie would be speaking. God answered prayer, and the young woman in question was among the 130 at the brunch. No sooner had she driven home, following the brunch, than she picked up the phone and said, "Mother, I want you to come right over. I want to know more about the way to find Jesus Christ."

The mother-in-law arrived very quickly, and after talking to her daughter-in-law, the latter prayed to receive Christ. The brunch guests that morning had worn butterfly nametags which they were asked to give to Millie if they had prayed to receive Christ, and now the young woman got off her knees after praying and said, "Now I'm going to send Millie Dienert my butterfly!"

One of the most successful pre-crusade events was a musical concert presented by George Beverly Shea, soloist, and Tedd Smith, pianist, in the Anaheim Convention Center. A packed-out crowd of seven thousand persons attended, and it was obvious that Crusade enthusiasm was mounting. The Santa Ana *Register* reported, SHEA'S CONCERT DEEPLY MOVES AUDIENCE WHO AWAIT CRUSADE!

At a breakfast gathering Billy addressed sixteen hundred business and civic leaders of Orange County. He urged them to "ring the bells of hope, faith, and righteousness" as they strive to cope with today's problems.

Amidst the mounting tensions in the world, Billy asserted, the old message he preached was more relevant to today than at any time in the history of the human race. Referring to his world travels, the evangelist shared the fact that he has found pessimism, fear, despair, and a vast lack of hope among the peoples of the world. But he himself believed there is hope and a way out of the mess society seems to be in.

"The way toward peace," Billy warned, "is blocked by the 'singers of siren songs.' The first siren song is that peace will automatically come to the world. . . . We cry peace, but there is no peace in our world. . . . Wars will continue to occur, because they come from our own greed and lust, and until man renovates his own human nature, peace will be a fleeting thing. Our problem is a heart problem, and until we straighten out the heart of man, we're going to have trouble. . . . The individual must get his heart right with God and his neighbor if he wants to contribute to peace. . . . It costs more than money. This kind of contribution will mean discipline, reading the Bible, praying, and making our contribution in society as a true Christian."

The second siren song Dr. Graham cited was the erroneous idea that we can ignore social problems and expect they will eventually go away. "We have a race problem and a poverty problem . . . both of these pale beside the drug and pornography problems facing our country. . . ."

Again, Dr. Graham did not blame young people for the breakdown in morality, but pointed his finger at the older generation. "The young people are only victims." He said this breakdown in morality could lead to a failure of American democracy. "Very few true democracies in the world survive when morality becomes weak. . . . When we take God out of our schools, the prayers out of the schools, and give the young people no more moral teaching, a vacuum develops."

The third siren song of today, Dr. Graham maintained, is the empty hope that economic utopianism is the answer to everything we need. "We have made the mistake of thinking that man is only mind and body. He is spirit too. By neglecting the spirit we have seen a breakdown of the total moral system. . . . We have given the young of today a caricature of Christianity . . . some of their favorite sayings like 'drop out' and 'tune in' are really religious expressions.

"We know the young are substituting sex and drugs for God and a personal relationship to Him through Jesus Christ. . . . They're doing their thing, but missing the real thing. . . . American society is trying to live on things, but it can't do it and has consequently come to believe in the fourth siren song, the claim that problems are completely insoluble. . . . This is patently false. . . . Although many people are pessimistic about the world's chances for survival, the Bible is a book of optimism. . . .

"The answer to the world's problems is the second coming of Christ. . . . The God who helped us in the past will help us today if we will only listen and heed. We must keep the bells of hope, faith, and righteousness ringing."

Other pre-crusade appearances included a conference with newsmen where he gave rapid-fire answers to questions ranging from theology to Vietnam; and a reception for team members and the executive committee, their wives, and other workers hosted by Claude W. Edwards, chairman of the board of Alpha Beta Acme Markets.

But the one event that surpassed everyone's expectations was the Ruth Graham luncheon — how do you serve meals to eleven thousand women at one time?

13

Women in the Arena

A woman walked out of Anaheim Convention Center on September 15 and was heard to say: "I never dreamed that I would see the day when eleven thousand women would leave a building with New Testaments in their hands. How heart-moving!"

The moving of hearts began in early July when Harry Williams began inviting women to be a part of a committee to plan a luncheon at which Mrs. Billy Graham would speak. Rare indeed are Ruth Graham's personal appearances, and even more rare her acceptance of speaking invitations. When word reached southern California that the lovely wife of the evangelist had responded favorably to the invitation of her long-time friend, Mary Ann Mooney, to address a luncheon gathering, the ripple of good news spread fast.

Mrs. James B. Sheets, chairman of the luncheon, and Mrs. Frank Pittman, reservations chairman, have spearheaded the organization of many large southern California functions, but never had they attempted anything on the scale of this luncheon at the Convention Center. Before the event they recorded 11,000 reservations and declined an estimated 5,000. Some called it the largest group ever served at one time west of the Mississippi — including Texas!

How do you seat 11,000 women in a half hour? Organization was the key. Mrs. Sheets hit upon the idea of color coordination to guide the women to their reserved places in Exhibition Hall and the adjacent Arena. Color-coordinated signs matched luncheon table colors, and hostesses wore banners of the same color as their area. Guests were met by "crowd control people" who directed them by their tickets to the corresponding color area. Within half an hour 11,000 women were seated with their hostesses, awaiting the program.

What do you feed 11,000 discriminating women? George Seelt, food and beverage director for Szado Foods, recommended a menu of fresh fruit salad. The food served ran into staggering proportions: 540 pounds kumquats; 1,400 frozen melon balls; 2,000 pounds crenshaw melons; 500 pounds grapes; 750 pounds sliced peaches; 2,000 pounds (1 ton!) cottage cheese; 16,000 strawberries; plus 900 gallons coffee and 50 gallons of milk. The beautiful table decorations added up to 1,300 dozen roses, 500 mums, 150 yards garland, 3 gallons glue — and well covered but well appreciated were a couple hundred blisters!

At each place was a gold-wrapped New Testament, tied with green ribbons. Mrs. Paul Robbins and twenty-five helpers wrapped the gift Testaments that made a lasting memento of the event.

Special guests with Mrs. Graham at the head table were: Mrs. Ronald Reagan, California's First Lady who served as honorary chairman; Mrs. James B. Sheets; Mrs. Earl Mooney; Mrs. Fred Dienert, acting as Mistress of Ceremonies; Norma Zimmer, singer from the Lawrence Welk TV program; Miss Ethel Waters, grand old lady of Gospel song; Mrs. Don Nixon, sister-in-law of President Nixon; area prayer chairmen for the crusade; and this writer.

Governor Reagan's wife graciously welcomed the women and said the event was a deserved tribute to Ruth Graham and a great honor for California. Crusade pianist Tedd Smith accompanied Miss Waters and Norma Zimmer, each of whom received a rousing ovation for her message in song. Miss Waters, now seventy-three, appears infrequently these days and she voiced gratitude to her Savior for allowing her the privilege, as she put it, "of standing in front of you and proclaiming my wonderful Jesus' love . . . and to do this for my precious child Billy and his darling girl Ruth."

Norma Zimmer confided: "I don't speak often and when I attempt to speak butterflies set in . . . but I would like to tell you what's in my heart. I never raise my voice in song without asking the Lord to let me be an instrument of His love. Before every television show that I do, I find a quiet spot and ask God to let me bring joy into the audience's hearts. If I didn't have the Lord as my strength I wouldn't be able to go on, and I am so grateful."

The magnitude of the luncheon was beyond comprehension. Someone commented, "We all marvelled at the order and peacefulness that prevailed over the entire luncheon — seemingly impossible with that number of people."

A woman who had worked behind the scenes saw the intricately planned program unfold and exclaimed: "This is the most thrilling thing I have ever witnessed. The Lord had His hand in the whole thing."

The women had done a magnificent job, but they had not done it alone. Moments before entering, women stood in small clusters with heads bowed, praying before being ushered into the Hall and the Arena. Someone commented to Ruth Graham that it was a tremendous crowd, and Ruth smiled and said, "It could be frightening were it not for the fact that I know people have been and are praying."

It was vital preparation for Ruth Graham's stirring talk that followed.

14

Wives, Husbands, and God

Millie Dienert introduced Ruth Graham to the overflow luncheon audience with these words: "It has been said ofttimes that behind a great man is a great woman, and that term 'great' can be defined in different ways. Today, relative to our speaker, she is a great woman as a mother, with five children and the extra pressures of assuming dual parenthood whenever necessary. She is a great woman as a wife, because of the extra pressures that have been hers due to the prominence of her husband. Her husband has said of her: 'She is a woman of God.' The other day, her lovely daughter said to me: 'Mother is a good listener.' There is a great woman, whose husband believes she is a woman of God, whose children say that she is a good listener. And so, Mrs. Billy Graham, we are going to be good listeners."

I was one among the eleven thousand who listened well, and here, somewhat condensed, is Ruth's talk, which she described modestly as "suggestions that I have jotted down over the years to help and inspire me in the job at hand."

Sometime ago a friend of ours sent his son to a church-related school where he lost his faith in the religion department. Shortly after this his brother and sister-in-law, while on their honeymoon, were accidentally killed. Having no inner resources, this boy cracked up and had to be placed in a mental hospital. In contrast, when Dan and Mel Piatt were in Australia last year getting ready for Crusade meetings, their son and daughter-in-law and little grandson were killed in a head-on collision. They were sick at the time with malaria and couldn't get to the funeral. The little family was buried on Dan and Mel's 28th wedding anniversary. When I saw Dan in Oslo last spring, he said: "Ruth, this is the greatest, the most tremendous experience we have ever gone through. Not once has our faith in the goodness and the wisdom of God faltered. The hardest time is at night when we can't sleep. Then the Bible verses that we have memorized over the years come to sustain and strengthen us. All we ask of God is that He teach us everything that He wants us to learn from this experience."

Jesus said, "He that heareth my words and doeth them, him will I liken to the wise man which built his house upon the rock. And the rains descended and the floods came, and the winds blew and beat upon that house, and it fell not, for it was founded upon a rock. He that heareth these words of mine and doeth them not, him will I liken unto the foolish man which built his house upon the sand. And the rains descended and the floods came, and the winds blew and beat upon that house, and it fell, and great was the fall thereof."

An architect friend of ours in Florida told us that the Florida building code requires that a house be built to withstand the strongest hurricane, even though a hurricane might not come but once in ten years, if then. In Proverbs 14:1 we are told, "Every wise woman buildeth her house." John Trapp, in the seventeenth century, translated that: "Every holy and handy woman . . ." You and I both know some women who are holy, and they aren't particularly handy; and we know some who are handy and they aren't particularly holy. But this is God's combination: "Every holy and handy woman." Are we building our homes according to God's building code? Is our blueprint the Bible? Is our foundation Jesus Christ, Himself? Is the superstructure built as we hear His words and do them? The Bible is the most relevant, the most exciting, the most marvelously practical book in the world today.

When you begin to apply the Bible to your everyday life, you come up with some surprisingly practical solutions. You begin to change, your attitudes begin to change. Some time ago *Parents Magazine* did a survey on what kind of discipline develops a child's character the most: mild, permissive, or strict. They said that it didn't seem to make much difference. The thing that developed a child's character the most was the overall atmosphere in the home, particularly the attitude of the mother. What are our attitudes in our homes? Toward our husbands?

God, you know, created woman to be a help meet for her husband, not, as we slur it together, "helpmeet," but a help that is meet for her husband; in other words, a help suited to his needs, wishes, desires — tailor made, if you wish, with a few alterations now and then. My advice to any young girls who are not yet married is: Marry a man to whom you don't mind adjusting. God tailors a wife to fit her husband, not the other way around. We are told in the New Testament: "Wives, adapt yourselves to your own husbands." Marriage, as you know, is not necessarily a 50-50 proposition. Sometimes it is 100-0. And don't expect the impossible. Joan Winmill Brown in London commented to a reporter that some women expect their husbands to be to them what only Jesus Christ Himself can be. Remember, you married a man, not God. Stop thinking about what you wish your husband would be to you, and start concentrating on what you should be to your husband.

Have you studied your husband lately? What is he really like? What does he need? What does he want? If you were a man, what sort of a woman would you like to come home to at night? You may not be beautiful or glamorous or young anymore, and at night you may be too tired to care, but you can be loving and appreciative. Some time ago I saw a filling station in Las Vegas with a sign that said, "Free aspirin and sympathy." Now, are we going to let a filling station beat us at our game?

You say, "Yes, but you don't know my husband." No, I don't, but God does. The best advice I ever heard given to a woman with a difficult husband was: "Your business is to make him happy, not to make him good." You see, only God can make him good. We are to take care of the possible and trust God for the impossible. Many a woman I know has made herself miserable trying to do what she can't, while she makes her children miserable as she fails to do what she can.

Ask God to help you become the woman He wants you to be — a wife your husband needs and wants. It may involve a more realistic commitment to God, a more honest appraisal of yourself. This may involve appearance, thriftiness, better cooking, better managing, more neatness — or perhaps the opposite. I have a friend who drives her husband up the wall with her neatness. It may involve reading more or staying home more or talking less or listening with interest and appreciation or being more cheerful. I am convinced that cheerfulness is a habit — being more demonstrative, more aggressively loving. I remember the late Robert Quilan writing: "A happy marriage is the union of two good forgivers."

Our attitude toward our husbands will affect our children. As David Goodman said in his tremendous book, *A Parent's Guide to the Emotional Needs of Children*: "What children need most is two parents who love and appreciate one another, and who love and appreciate them. All-around love and appreciation in the home makes for more happiness and security." Do you love and appreciate your children? Do they know it?

It isn't easy growing up in today's world. Look at the world situation and the pressures on young people to conform, to be with it. Look at the materialistic, secularistic society and the false standard it creates. No moral absolutes. Instead of "Thou shalt not" it is "Why not?" Nothing is wrong so long as it is meaningful and doesn't hurt anyone — whatever that means.

All this is resulting in moral confusion, crime and violence, and laws that protect the criminal more than the victim. God is ignored, the Word of God is discredited, and faith is being destroyed all too often by men whose ordination vows bound them to uphold and proclaim both.

Our families are facing pressures, temptations, and problems that we never had to face as we were growing up. The dirt roads and horses and buggies of our parents' days have given way to the high-powered cars and freeways of today. A few months ago the road between the small town where we live and the neighboring city was widened from two lanes to four, and, in places, five. For a few weeks after the blacktop was laid we had no white dividing lines. Talk about a frightening experience — driving down a five-lane highway with no guidelines! On this unmarked stretch five people were killed in a head-on collision. And we turn our children loose on the freeways of life with no road signs, no traffic rules, no guardrails, no center lane, no dividing line, no speed limit, and no stop signs — in high-powered cars with faulty brakes! No wonder they have wrecks.

What must we teach our children today? We must teach them that God loves them and watches over them; that Jesus died to save them from their sins and rose again from the dead and will be with them always; that the Holy Spirit dwells in every believer to do for us what we cannot possibly do for ourselves. Teach them the Bible is the Word of God — their one sure guide in an unsure world. Teach them to learn it, to love it, and to live it. Especially teach them the heart of it, that "God so loved the world that he gave his only begotten Son, that whosoever believeth in him should not perish, but have everlasting life."

An actress in London asked me two years ago: "How do you explain the crucifixion to your children?" Exactly as the Bible does. God died for my sins. Whatever you do, don't underestimate or try to soften the horror or the glory of it. Children can grasp deep spiritual truths. They put us to shame, in fact. Children, for instance, understand that you love them, but not their dirt. They are welcome in the home on a rainy day, but not the mud. They also know that different stains require different treatment, and there is a stain on the souls of men that nothing could remove but the life blood of One who was completely pure and without sin. Only God could qualify. Had there been any other way, don't you think He would have taken it? So God became man and died for us. Teach them this fact, and that each one of us must face Him personally.

Teach them to pray. Teach them that they can call God collect and person-to-person anytime, anywhere; and teach them that our main goal in life is to please Him, not people. Especially if you live in a parsonage, don't sacrifice your children on the altar of public opinion. I have a friend who is more concerned about her children's manners than their morals. There are moral issues and there are nonmoral issues.

I was scolding our teenage son the night before last and he said: "Oh, Mom, don't get pushed out of shape over it." I had never heard that one before. But moral issues are the ones worth getting pushed out of shape over, and the nonmoral issues are the ones not worth getting pushed out of shape over. Among moral issues I would list honesty, obedience, respect, and reverence. Among nonmoral issues I would list matters of taste, fads, ordinary hazards of growing up such as noise, and accidents. If the Bible is specific on an issue, then there is no question about its rightness or wrongness, but where the Bible is not specific, be very careful before you say: "Thou shalt not." Don't confuse your prejudices with your convictions.

How do we teach our children? First of all, by example. Someone has said that the best way to get a child to eat is to let him see the parents enjoying their food. Do you enjoy God? Man's chief end, as we all know, is to glorify God and enjoy Him forever. Man's chief end is not personal happiness. It is not success. It is not having what we want in life. Man's chief end is to glorify God and to enjoy Him forever. Then, irrespective of the circumstances, happiness does follow. Do you delight yourself in the Lord, as we are told in Psalm 37:4? I prefer the Septuagint translation: "Indulge yourself with delight in the Lord." If you enjoy God, you will enjoy prayer and you will enjoy your

Bible study. And it will show. You can't hide it. If you don't enjoy it, that will show too. And you can't fool a kid.

Did you see the cartoon where the little boy says to his mother: "When I do it, it's temper; and when you do it, it's nerves"? Some time ago our 11-year-old son said to me: "Mom, is Zsa Zsa Gabor a wicked woman?" Before I had a chance to say, "I do not know Miss Gabor," he replied, "I mean, Mom, does she get cross?"

Think it through! "Does she get cross?" Henry Drummond spoke of irritability as the "vice of the virtuous." Nothing sours people on Christianity more quickly than sour Christians. F. B. Meyer once said: "We may doubt the reality of any blessing that does not make us sweeter and easier to get along with, especially at home."

And we must teach children day by day and little by little. The Bible says: "Line upon line, precept upon precept; here a little, there a little." In Solomon's prayer he asked the Lord: "Give thy servant an understanding heart." The Hebrew word means a hearing heart. How can we be understanding unless we listen and know when to quit talking?

We must be quick to praise and slow to blame. In Psalm 72:15, King David said of his son Solomon, "Prayer also shall be made for him continually, and daily shall he be praised." Do you pray for your children continually? And do you praise them daily?

Some time ago when the Dienerts and Bill and I were vacationing in Jamaica, Bill got the wild idea that he and I should learn to water-ski. I never did master skiing, but I got some terrific pointers on child training. Our instructor kept his instruction simple. And he encouraged. He taught us how to balance, then he turned loose. I thought, if only we parents would keep our instructions simple, teach our children how to balance, and know when to turn loose. Sometimes the turning loose is the hardest part.

I once heard an illustration of an apple tree. In April the apple tree looks absolutely dead and bare. In May you will have it loaded with beautiful blossoms. In July, August, or September, depending on the kind of tree, you will have delicious apples ready to eat. But don't expect apples in April. In April an apple tree is perfect for an apple tree in April. In May it is perfect for an apple tree in May. In June, July, and August it is perfect for an apple tree in those months. Don't expect too much too soon.

There is a roadsign on the highway I mentioned earlier that has a message I want copied on my tombstone. It simply said: "End of construction; thank you for your patience."

Now, you may already be perfect, or you may just think you are, but be honest. Most of us are like the old witch in "Snow White and the Seven Dwarfs." We look in the mirror and say: "Mirror, mirror on the wall, who is fairest of them all?" hoping the mirror will say, "You." But all we see is an old witch. Now can God take old witches like us and make us what He wants us to be? Yes, if we let Him. We bring Him our sin, our mistakes, and our messed-up lives. He alone can forgive and transform. In Jesus' day, Bartimaeus came with his blindness, Zaccheus with his crookedness, Mary Magdalene with her seven devils; Lazarus, you may remember, didn't come at all. Jesus went to him.

If it is possible to have a favorite hymn, I think mine would be, "Come ye sinners, poor and needy, weak and weary, sick and sore; Jesus, waiting, stands to help you, full of pity, love and power; Let not conscience bid you linger, nor of fitness fondly dream; All the fitness He requires is to feel your need of Him" . . .

Our Father, thank You for being here. You know there is someone here who is carrying a load too heavy for her. There is someone for whom life has become unbearable, someone who is trying to escape reality through drugs and too much alcohol. When the fog clears, there is reality still staring her in the face. Only, Lord, each time she is a little less able to cope with it. And there is someone here who has to live with problems that can't be solved because there is no solution, some haunted by a tragedy they can never forget, some enslaved by sin they can neither escape nor control, bored by purposelessness and worn out by drudgery. There are some who are tired and discouraged and ready to quit. Lord, help each one to remember that all the fitness You require is to feel our need of You. So, as the blind came in Your day, the sick, the impure, the bitter, the weary, the confused, so may we also come just as we are. Forgive us, please; make us clean and whole. Take us into Your family, and as we leave here we will know that we will never again be alone nor unloved for You will go with us. You will never leave us nor forsake us, and nothing can ever separate us from Your love. Make us Your eager pupils. May we hear Your words and do them. As we do, we know You will make us sweeter and easier to get along with, especially at home. In Jesus' Name, Amen.

15

Building a Crusade

The Anaheim Crusade and its transformation of thousands of Angelinos began several years earlier in the hearts of concerned Christians. One was Dave Messenger, M.D., who saw the new stadium taking shape and immediately pictured Billy Graham at the pitcher's mound with all Orange County — and more — getting into the game. He wrote the Rev. Robert H. Schuller, pastor of Garden Grove Community Church, and received a phone call in response. "I couldn't answer by mail. Your idea is tremendous. Yes, we must try to get Billy Graham to the Angel Stadium." The two men devised a plan of action and agreed to pray for God's leading.

For Lorin Griset, mayor of thriving Santa Ana, the Crusade dream began at the time of the Los Angeles Crusade in 1963. The hope crystallized when he received a telephone call from Dr. Messenger about his talk with Bob Schuller. Griset joined them in praying, and shortly after, the three organized an Invitational Committee comprising 125 pastors throughout Orange County who began promoting the project.

Crusade momentum picked up when Mrs. Earl Mooney, a college classmate of Ruth Graham, invited the Grahams to a Northern Orange County Christian Women's Club dinner. It was to be Men's Night at the Disneyland Hotel August 23, 1965, and Billy agreed to address the group. The Grahams spent the day with the Mooneys, and as they drove past the Angel Stadium that afternoon, the Mooneys commented that it would be a wonderful place for a Crusade and they hoped Billy would consider coming back to Orange County for that purpose someday. About a thousand people attended the dinner, and when Billy invited listeners to commit their lives to Christ about three hundred raised their hands. An editorial in the Fullerton *Daily News Tribune* called the dinner "the most inspirational evening in the history of Orange County." It gave Billy a glimpse of both the needs and opportunities in the fastest-growing county in the country.

Because he is a real man with a real message, Billy Graham gets many invitations to lead Crusades. None of them are ignored, but most must be refused. Queries, hopes, suggestions, and actual invitations come from around the world at the current unbelievable rate of seven hundred a month — enough to keep Billy going morning, noon, and night for two hundred years. Why did Billy select Orange County for a concentrated effort?

A *Look* magazine article revealed part of the reason. It quoted Graham as saying religion needed to make more of an impact in suburban life, and that he was planning his first suburban campaign in Anaheim, California, in 1969. Dr. Walter Smyth, Graham's Director of Crusades, and associate evangelist Grady Wilson met with officials of the stadium and the Invitational Committee members in May 1968 to express Graham's desire to come. Within no time an Executive Committee was organized and functioning smoothly with Team member Harry Williams in charge as the Southern California Crusade Director.

In November enthusiasm and energy began to flow outward as the Rev. Arvid F. Carlson, a minister in the city of Orange, became chairman of the Crusade Prayer Committee. The strategy was to work through existing structures as much as possible, delegating work to key people in the area.

Mary Ann Mooney was named women's prayer chairman, and she promoted prayer through such groups as Christian Women's Clubs, women's Bible classes, area church women's meetings, and home prayer meetings. She chose ten area chairmen who selected several district chairmen who in turn chose zone chairmen. The latter named neighborhood leaders who contacted Crusade prayer chairmen in the churches. These ladies found women who would open their homes once a week between August 18 and October 6 and serve as prayer hostesses.

John Adams was named to enlist prayer support among laymen. He contacted Christian Businessmen's Committees, the Gideons, International Christian Leadership groups, civic leaders, service organizations, denominational men's fellowships, and individuals in industry, business, and the military. Nearly three hundred men's prayer groups promised support. At the Douglas Aircraft Company's Long Beach plant, seventeen prayer groups were organized.

The youth division, under the Rev. Bob Ohman, secured the cooperation of such groups as Youth for Christ, Campus Life, Inter-Varsity, Campus Crusade, Young Life, Christian Endeavor, youth fellowships in cooperating churches, various Christian colleges and schools in southern California and sixty-five summer campgrounds. The surprisingly high attendance of youth at the Crusade was attributable in large part to the prayer volume focused here.

The Rev. Galal Gough, chairman of the Ministers' Council, rallied prayer support in the churches. He organized ministers' breakfasts and luncheons and encouraged the appointment of prayer chairmen in the churches. Graham's tract on prayer went to thousands of Christians who immediately began their intercessory support of the Crusade.

On June 12, 1969, a missionary executive luncheon attracted twenty missionary agency leaders. These leaders informed their field personnel of the Crusade and received assurance of global prayer reinforcements.

The Rev. Armin Gesswein, Crusade associate, toured missionary conferences in Hong Kong, Formosa, and Japan distributing prayer booklets and explaining the upcoming

Crusade. The far-flung efforts stirred responses from Christian laymen and mission leaders around the world. One said, "You may inform the Crusade that in this Caribbean area there has been established a prayer group with the 'burden of concern' of exactly 133 faithful and very devout Christians. . . . You shall see God do mighty things. Amen!" Other letters told of fasting and praying for Crusade results.

During the month of June, Mr. Gesswein conducted three Schools of Prayer in the southern California area. On September 7 an insert in church bulletins pictured the evangelist and his exhortation: "Please pray fervently . . . and participate faithfully . . . ," with the dates and information about the Crusade.

In the final seven weeks preceding the Crusade, prayer intensified as approximately 4,600 homes opened for 30-minute prayer meetings morning or evening once a week. "Prayer Time," a quarter-hour Crusade radio program, was broadcast on four stations.

Joining in all the prayer support was a woman who describes herself as "the original little old lady from Pasadena." Others call her "Billy Graham's Prayer Warrior."

Eighty-five-year-old Mrs. Pearl Goode, despite painful arthritis and a troublesome heart, has attended forty-three of Billy Graham's Crusades all over the world. Mrs. Goode was a nurse in San Marino in 1949 when she picked up a newspaper and read an article about a young evangelist preaching in Los Angeles. That night she attended the Crusade on the corner of Washington Boulevard and Hill Street. The Crusade was extended to eight weeks and Mrs. Goode attended almost every night. God spoke to her through Billy's messages and she told God, "I want to devote my life to following Billy Graham and praying for him."

How does an elderly widow with slender financial means get to numerous distant Crusades? "The Lord provides, and every time it's a miracle — just one miracle after another," she answers. And prayers and miracles of various kinds seemed to characterize the Crusade from the first heart prayer to the final heart response — which hasn't yet been recorded.

16

Like a Loving Army

Gloria and Nick glanced up at the shabby building, looked at each other dubiously and hesitantly stepped inside. Could someone really live above this bar? they wondered as they climbed the creaking stairs. They knocked on a door. An elderly lady opened the door a crack. She appeared frightened at having callers. Politely the couple invited the woman to the Billy Graham Crusade. The response was guarded, noncommittal. She may have been conned too many times by engaging visitors.

Gloria and Nick were cooperating in a door-to-door visitation campaign preceding the Anaheim Crusade. Some 175,000 people had volunteered to hand out Crusade literature on September 21. It was an eye-opening experience for Gloria and Nick.

As members of a large downtown church in Santa Ana that is surrounded by business and commercial ventures, Gloria and Nick had little acquaintance with the real neighborhood of people. As they moved along their designated route, they came to a very old home with several mailboxes in front. They knocked and waited. This time the door was opened wide enough for them to see inside. They were not prepared to see such stark living in the shadow of their church.

A rickety table stood in the center of the room. There was a dilapidated couch along one wall and paper strewn over the bare floor. They saw a hotplate on which, apparently, food was cooked.

After giving an invitation to the Crusade and leaving literature, they made their way to the rear of the property where, they were told, an old man lived. Surely their informant must be mistaken. The only building they could see was a decrepit shack which looked as though a strong wind would cave it in. They approached the shack with misgivings.

A very old man answered their timid knock. What they saw inside made the previous sight encouraging by comparison. Another table, much more rickety than the first one, a rusty, sagging army cot and a dirty light bulb on a frayed ceiling cord presided over a dirt floor. Here, too, they left an invitation.

The visitors departed, sadder but wiser about the woes of their neighbors. Their church already operated a program at a store front in this area, but their interest up to this point had been of a purely social concern. Now a new dimension of love and compassion would be added.

The Rev. Paul C. Johnson of Orange had the task of organizing these working "walkers." Mr. Johnson first called ministers together for prayer and planning. They mapped out boundaries for visitation assignments and went back to begin a truly immense effort.

Mr. Johnson was really sold on the program. "It was an opportunity for church pastors and laymen to become involved in a dynamic plan to revive the religious interest of their neighbors and friends. My own congregation came back so enthusiastic after that Sunday afternoon of walking. It provided the impetus to get them to the Crusade and to be busy about inviting others."

The Reverend Galal Gough organized ministers through area, district, and zone chairmen. They transmitted messages about prayer groups, Christian Life and Witness classes, Bible discussion groups, visitation committees, and usher and choir training that quickly reached three thousand people. Early in the venture Mr. Gough cherished the hope that this would ultimately result in a renewal of the ministry throughout southern California. After the Crusade, he looked back and observed: "While our work pointed toward a year-long program of evangelism, from the moment we began we could see that it sparked a revival of confidence and commitment to evangelism, in addition to new spiritual life and prayer growth among the ministers which was to be felt in hundreds of congregations by thousands of people."

Some four thousand Bible discussion leaders were trained from churches throughout southern California. The objective was to have study groups established wherever possible to which inquirers at the Crusade could come for instruction. Robert H. Jones, who until August 1968 was an executive with the Carnation Company, headed this strategic training program.

Helping to spearhead interest by laymen in the Leadership Training Classes was Dr. David H. Paynter, chairman of the Council of Laymen. Dr. Paynter explained: "Church members who had not been active in their own churches were offered opportunities to become involved. And members of various churches benefited through better communications with each other. We need this personal involvement in our churches more than ever before, and the Billy Graham Crusade helped to make this possible. We wanted the Crusade to be more than a series of nightly meetings. If the event were to have a penetrating and lasting effect upon our communities, people had to be informed, interested, and inspired."

These objectives remained before the people before, during, and then after the Crusade, even as this book was being written.

During the Crusade a daily School of Evangelism was conducted by such well-known and eminently qualified people as: the Rev. Cliff Barrows; Dr. Kenneth L. Chafin; Dr. Robert O. Ferm; Dr. Leighton Ford; the Rev. Howard O.

Jones; the Rev. D. James Kennedy; Mr. Charles Riggs; Dr. Wilbur M. Smith; Dr. Walter Smyth, and Dr. Grady Wilson. Dr. Victor B. Nelson was Director of the School which brought together hundreds of pastors, seminary students, and church workers interested in imparting the Gospel message to others.

The Crusade organization tapped the energies and talents of thousands of young and old, laymen and clergy, and members of various denominations. About two thousand ushers alone were recruited, and four hundred to five hundred were on duty every night of the Crusade.

One of them, Paul, was the head usher in his church, and his pastor asked him to assist at the Crusade. "If it works out with my time schedule, and if it's convenient, I'll go," Paul agreed reluctantly.

Then Paul decided to go to the first Crusade meeting. He was surprised and impressed. The next night he went again, and the next, and so on for all ten services. On the final Sunday afternoon Paul walked forward to make a decision. The following Sunday at a special laymen's service in his own church, Paul related his experience. No one could have been more surprised than his pastor to see his head usher taking this open stand.

Crusades such as this cost a lot of money! The Anaheim Crusade, like other Graham Crusades, was financed and conducted by laymen and clergymen of the area. Finance Chairman was Ray L. Smith, executive vice president and director of a southern California bank. The $585,150 budget adopted by the committee covered an eighteen-month period, including the pre-crusade preparations, the Crusade services, and a lengthy period of follow-up. The evangelist did not receive remuneration for his part. Smith commented on his own role: "Finances are the means to an end — I am much more concerned and interested in the spiritual end, but somebody has to do this phase of the work also, and so there were some of us who were willing to offer our services for that reason."

Smith and others who raised and handled the half million dollars believed the people of southern California would receive rich benefits from their giving — a more spiritual environment, a drawing together of Christians who cooperated, and a renewed spirit of faith and understanding in individuals.

Crusade director Harry Williams was gratified at the results. "The philosophy of a Crusade concerns the number of lives changed and the spiritual activation of local congregations," he commented. "Crusades are ultimately designed to mobilize the whole Church to reach the whole community. Ten to fifteen years from now we'll still be hearing what has happened during these days and during this past year of preparation."

17

Very Special People

Jessica Shaver's Volvo looked like a toy car on the asphalt expanse surrounding the gigantic Anaheim Angel Stadium. Every time she entered the vast parking lot as she arrived for work, she tried to visualize the bustle and excitement when the Crusade would be actually underway.

The Crusade quarters were tucked away on the third floor above the baseball team offices. How well Jessica remembered her first introduction to what had now become familiar. Early in December 1968 she had come to the Crusade office to apply for a job. Eight people, eight desks and typewriters, piles of boxes, files, stationery, receipts, bulletins, and personal belongings crowded two small rooms. Here, one whole year before the Crusade was scheduled to begin, the embryonic plans had been taking shape.

Financial donations were coming in; someone had to acknowledge them. Local Christians were writing for details about neighborhood prayer groups, counseling requirements, choir rehearsals, and seeking information as to how they could help. There were countless letters to be typed, calls to be made, and appointments to set up.

In another, much larger room, Tone Ferry kept unpaid volunteers sending out mailings to southern California ministers, to the neophyte committees being organized, to council chairmen, and the general Christian public.

It was plain to see, Jessica mused, that more help was needed. She wondered where she would fit in. There were others who came in those early days, some in September 1968.

Before long all positions had been filled, and by January 2, 1969, the rough, unfinished walls, piles of sawdust, crude doorways, and expressionless rooms had given way to attractive decor with avocado green carpets. The windows of the offices offered a panorama of Orange County from above the stadium's main entrance.

Jessica found the correspondence most interesting. Letters such as this: "How this state needs a revival that will stir it from center to circumference!" "God bless all of you as we mentally keep a circle of God's love around you and your wonderful work." "Many nights my head never touches the pillow! We are on a 24-hour prayer chain from our church, carrying the work of the Crusade office to the throne of grace constantly."

The non-salaried volunteer workers came from almost every Protestant denomination in southern California as well as from the Roman Catholic Church. Many were older people, but six colleges and universities and twenty-four high schools were also represented. The young people's straight hair, cut-off blue jeans, sandals, football jerseys, mini-skirts and bell-bottom slacks contrasted with the demure apparel of older women, some of whom wore hats, and the pin-striped suits and polished black shoes of retired executives.

The volunteers came from various walks of life, including teachers, nurses, salesladies, secretaries, court-reporters, telephone operators, and a wealthy oil operator and an FBI agent. Many of them journeyed once a week from as far away as Inglewood and the San Fernando Valley, more than sixty miles.

There was an emergency-on-call list of workers who could be reached day or night when a rush job was unexpectedly needed. Crusade officials termed these the elite of elite.

One church had a group who worked every Thursday night. These people, mostly couples, held regular jobs during the daytime so could volunteer their help only in the evening. They called themselves the Lamplighters. Others acquired descriptive names representing something unique about themselves. "Faithful" became the title for Alda Kryder and Helen Barbre who spent at least four hours a day in the Crusade office.

The workers, paid and volunteer, learned that a Crusade is planned as meticulously as a military invasion! This small army helped to prepare Crusade bulletins, ministers' information packets and assorted letters which poured out of the office every week. By August 17, 1969, one month previous to the Crusade, some ten thousand people — one from as far away as Kenai, Alaska, another from Ann Arbor, Michigan, others from Oklahoma City and Omaha, Nebraska — had put in a combined total of 60,636 man-hours of work. Before the Crusade closed, another 20,000 volunteers contributed an additional 200,000 man-hours.

In the southern California labor market, according to the State Employment Service, if these volunteers had been paid for their work it would have amounted to $781,908. The amount would have skyrocketed if volunteers were paid time and a half for night and weekend work, especially if they belonged to some kind of Crusade Union.

Coordinating the volunteer office work were Tone Ferry and Erma Jean Van Roekel. Tone and Erma Jean explained procedures patiently and endlessly. They had to keep everyone busy without being dictatorial.

Lillian Upsher has volunteered her help in fifteen Crusades to date. She lives in Oklahoma City when she isn't working at a Crusade. Her interest dates back to 1956 when her church participated in a local Crusade. She took her vacation in St. Paul in 1961 when Billy was holding a Crusade and volunteered her help there. "This is the best vacation I've ever had," she said afterward. She managed to take her vacations every year after that when a Crusade was underway: 1962, Chicago; 1963, Los Angeles; 1964, Columbus, Ohio, and Omaha, Nebraska; 1965, Hawaii; and then Copenhagen, Denmark; Houston, Texas; London, England; Kansas City, Kansas; San Antonio, Texas; New York again; and finally Anaheim. "Life for me really began in 1956 at that Crusade," she says. For her and many others, real life can be traced to an encounter with Christ at such Crusades.

Tone and Erma Jean got to know the regular volunteers intimately. They kept track of their families and often asked prayer in morning devotions for volunteers who faced surgery or other needs. The two women also devised a new color-coded filing system which the Graham Team will use in subsequent Crusades.

A casual visitor to Anaheim Stadium during the year preceding the Crusade might have expected the evangelist to appear momentarily if the high-geared activity were any indication. Harry Williams termed the "Big A" Stadium the cleanest, most well organized stadium the Graham Team had ever worked in. Billy later commented he had never seen such an efficiently operated Crusade office. Around Anaheim Stadium, it was easy to draw the conclusion that volunteers were very special people.

Someone who regarded them as very special was a golden-haired young lady who worked earnestly among them a few days before the Crusade opened. Who was she? She resembled her father, though many of the other workers didn't realize she was Miss Ruth "Bunny" Graham, Billy's daughter. What was her reaction to her surroundings?

Gracious and soft-spoken, Bunny said, "This is like any Crusade because the people here are special people — like the little blind lady who comes in and works so hard. The people come in every day and work for nothing, and do it willingly and happily. It's a joy to work with them. Everyone here works hard and late, some even skip meals, but love the work. It is such a pleasure to be a part of them." When co-workers learned Bunny's identity, they came over to speak with her, which she enjoyed. Her wedding was then about two months away. Ted Dienert, the handsome, muscular son of Fred and Millie, was the fortunate man.

The couple plan to work with the Graham Team in addition to Ted's work in TV production.

Beverly Giese, secretary to accountant John Rogers, perhaps handled the nittiest gritty. She dealt with numbers and more numbers, receipting all the money that came into the office, making up daily, weekly, and monthly reports, and taking care of the needs of the Finance Committee. Yet at the conclusion she said, "I hate to see it end . . . it's been a great job and I can't think of anywhere else that anyone here would like to work . . . just Christian fellowship and working for the Lord."

The morning that Billy Graham came to the office to personally thank the volunteers was a high point for everyone. Jessica felt almost as excited as the first time she'd attempted to type from the dictation machine and thought she was transcribing Cantonese — it turned out she just had the dictabelt in the machine the wrong way around!

Billy moved among the volunteers, shaking hands, visiting, and then said, "Many people have been involved in the preparation for this Crusade, preparation the audience is not aware of. I feel I have very little to do with it because I haven't done anything except prepare some sermons. . . . This has been a labor of love on your part and we're very grateful to you. I cannot properly thank you — that's what the judgment seat of Christ will be all about, for the Bible says every man will then have his praise of God. And that's going to be a wonderful occasion. You're serving the Lord Jesus Christ, and He will give you proper reward."

Jessica looked around. The looks on the faces were something to see. She was glad she was a part of it. Glad and thankful.

18

Co-Labor Corps and Number 817

Mrs. F. Howell, Co-Labor Corps volunteer, worked into the wee hours of the morning many nights during the Crusade. One evening toward the latter part of the week she arrived at the parking lot early to avoid heavy freeway traffic. It was an opportune time, she decided, to catch up on some sleep. Settling back comfortablly in her car seat she dozed off immediately. The next thing she knew she awoke, startled. It was very dark. Getting her bearings took a few moments, and then she glanced at her watch: it was 11 o'clock! Exhausted, she had slept right through the evening service! When she reported this to the Co-Laborers, she said, "I was just like the disciples in Gethsemane. Now I know how they must have felt!"

Mrs. Howell was one of hundreds of diligent volunteer workers in the Co-Labor Corps department. Some 165 men, women, and students worked after each service at long tables above which hung signs designating specific areas of work. The big signs read: COLLECTING, STATISICS, CODING, SORTING, RESEARCH, DESIGNATION, CHECKERS, TYPISTS, STUFFERS, FINAL FILE. Most of these people worked until their particular job was finished each night — until nearly midnight for some and until 3 or 4 A.M. for others.

The Co-Labor Corps' work is a vital part of every Crusade, yet is perhaps the least understood. Without this department, the Crusade results might be ineffective or at best very incomplete.

What happens to those who come forward indicating they are making a first-time decision or are seeking assurance or are rededicating their lives to God? Some people criticize this phase of a Crusade, saying, "There is no good way of following through . . . how do they know how many people actually came forward?"

I found out the answer to this and other important questions by watching the Co-Laborers night after night and learning the intriguing story from Don Myers, chief of the Co-Labor group.

The first night of the Crusade, Myers said, a man appeared in the Crusade offices and asked how he could find a particular decision card when it came through. Myers asked why he wanted the information, and the man explained that he and his wife were so concerned for the salvation of a friend that they had written personal letters to sixty churches and many friends asking for prayer that this woman would come to the Crusade and make a decision.

Myers felt this man was God's answer to his own prayer. He already had ten supervisors for ten of the eleven strategic sections for keeping records on follow-up of individual decisions. To make the system function, he still needed a Final Filing Captain. Myers showed the vistor, Bob, the numerical filing system and determined that the woman's number would be 817 if she signed a counselor's decision card. Bob promptly accepted the offered filing job, and Number 817 became a nightly watchword for the Co-Labor crew.

Myers himself, after being asked to head up the volunteer Co-Labor Corps, had taken a day off from his regular work to fly to New York at his own expense to learn the job. That was his own decision — he felt he could grasp the operation better by watching it done at the New York Crusade in May. So he spent fourteen hours on planes, going a circuitous route to save money, six hours in ground transportation and nine hours following the Co-Labor Chief around. He came back with six pages of valuable notes and a reputation as "that nut who went to New York"!

The epithet didn't bother Myers. Results were what counted, and Number 817 — among many others — was important.

"Collections" was the first section to handle the decision cards. "Runners" with red ribbons on their badges collected a batch of decision cards from advisors on the field and rushed them to the Co-Labor work area where they were recorded. The cards then went to "Statistics."

The second section gleaned such statistics as the type of decision, and the sex, age, and occupation of the counselee. These facts were recorded and continually tabulated on charts.

Next was "Coding." The man in charge of coding used the McBee numerical system and assigned a number for each combination of letters of the alphabet so a card could be filed numerically instead of alphabetically and thus be retrieved more easily. The coders put the number in the corner of the card and passed it to "Sorting."

Sorting workers scanned the cards for a complete church address. If the information given by the counselee was not complete, the card was sent to "Research."

The Research area used denominational and telephone and zip-code directories to complete the address and add other information which would guide the report to its appropriate destination. If there was no clue as to denominational preference or background, the card went to "Designation."

In Designation a group of ministers checked the geographical location and designated a specific church and minister to whom to send the decision report. Then it went to the first group of "Checkers."

Checkers examined the card three times to see if the address was legible and information complete for typists to type.

"Typists" recorded the inquirer's name and minister's name and address on a four-part NCR form so it showed through a window envelope. The typing was checked for accuracy and neatness — no strikeovers allowed.

Next, "Stuffers" separated #1 and #2 copies from the others and stuffed them into envelopes that contain return envelopes and a cover letter explaining what the receiving minister is expected to do. The envelopes were alphabetically sorted by church to avoid multiple mailings when possible. The envelopes went out the same night — sometimes at 2 or 3 A.M. — asking the ministers to make a personal follow-up call on the individual who made a decision.

"If the Crusade office doesn't hear from the pastor on a return form within ten days, copy #3 goes as a reminder," Myers explained. "If there is still no response within another ten days, the Crusade office makes a complete new set from the #4 copy, selects another minister and starts over to try to get a personal call made. The #3 and #4 copies and the original decision card go to the "Final File." This also contains the ministers' reports after they come back.

During the morning after every service, a volunteer crew types envelopes for letters from Billy Graham to the inquirers. There are two each for children and adults, the first letter going out within four days and the second in ten days.

The Co-Labor Corps work was not without its times of fun. There was the night the cake disappeared! The cook in the stadium kitchen had baked a big, beautiful cake with chocolate icing for the late-late workers. When it came time for refreshments, Myers announced the event over the microphone and picked up the cake box. It was surprisingly light; no cake!

Myers was pleased when his Deputy Chief and the FBI man in charge of Coding volunteered to take the case. After painstaking investigation the case was solved — with the evidence tending to incriminate the FBI man! The huge cake was then enjoyed by all, especially the triumphant representative of law and order!

Motto for the Co-Laborers was: "Count It All Joy," from

James 1:2. Many times they reminded each other of this. Lori Becker and her daytime Co-Laborers really put the motto to the test when, on the morning following a windstorm, they arrived to find the Co-Labor department covered with thick, red dust. Research papers were strewn everywhere, desks were covered with a thick film of dust, typewriters complained grittily. Southern California had had one of its unscheduled "Santanas," called "devil winds" by oldtimers. "We weren't going to let this defeat us," Lori cheerfully explained, "so we just set to work getting rid of the dust with a vacuum cleaner, and the workers kept right on working. We'd say, 'Lift up your typewriter,' and they would."

Don Myers said, "I think the devil tried to deposit most of the infield in the Co-Labor room — but that was the day the work crew turned out double their usual amount when there were more decision cards to process than at any other time during the Crusade!" Counting it all joy had made the difference!

Dave Clauson, in charge of Statistics, had tried unsuccessfully three times before the Crusade to get his vacation lined up for the weeks of the Crusade. So during the Crusade Dave worked at his regular job, then rushed to the Crusade and stayed late. He had three or four twenty-hour days in a row. "Oddly enough," he revealed, "I wasn't tired. I was going on 'Jesus-power.' " And Dave had been a Christian less than one year!

The highest ratio of decisions to attendance in any Graham Crusade, 5.3 percent, was recorded at this Crusade. There were 11,888 women and girls and 8,448 men and boys who came forward. Of that number 9,881 were first-time decisions.

But what about Number 817? At the conclusion of God's ten days in the Anaheim Stadium, no counselor's card showed Number 817, and many were disappointed. Hadn't God heard? Had the recording system failed?

The Co-Labor Corps was not discouraged. Its work contributed incalculably to the lives of the inquirers. And

God's Crusade is not ended, nor concerned Christians' prayers repudiated. They go on, with prevailing intercession for Number 817 and for others with God's appointed number — by those who are co-laborers together with him.

19

Billy on TV

People across the country "visited" the Crusade by means of television, enjoying the music and hearing the good news of salvation from Billy Graham. One of Billy's more memorable sermons described the Judgment Day of God which every person will face. Here is a condensed version of that graphic message.

I am reading from 2 Peter 2 in a translation called *Good News for Modern Man*. I assure you it is good news, though it may sound fearful.

"For God did not spare the angels who sinned, but threw them into hell, where they are kept chained in darkness, waiting for the Day of Judgment. God did not spare the ancient world, but brought the Flood on the world of wicked men; the only ones he saved were Noah, who preached righteousness, and seven other people. God condemned the cities of Sodom and Gomorrah, destroying them with fire, and made an example of them for the wicked, of what will happen to them. He rescued Lot, a good man, who was troubled by the immoral conduct of lawless men. For that good man, living among them, day after day saw and heard such things that his good heart was tormented by their evil deeds. And so the Lord knows how to rescue godly men from their trials, and how to keep the wicked under punishment for the Day of Judgment, especially those who follow their filthy bodily lusts and despise God's authority."

One of my friends talked with a man in Hollywood who said, "Isn't it interesting how the image of God has changed in the last few years?" Our concept and image of God may have changed, but God never changes. He is the one constant in the universe. The Bible says, quoting God, "I am the Lord God. I change not." The Bible says there is no variableness nor shadow from turning with God. In all these eons of time, God has not changed in the slightest.

I read about a farmer who placed on a weather vane the words, "God is love," and his neighbor asked him, "Does that mean that God's love changes like the wind?" And the farmer answered, "No, it means that God is love whichever way the wind blows."

God loves you whichever way the wind blows in your life, whatever your sin, however you've disobeyed the laws of God. God will love you to the very gate of hell.

The Bible says also that God's holiness never changes. God is righteous and that's the reason sin is so repugnant to Him. Sin is rebellion against God. Sin is wanting to do your own will instead of God's will, and the Bible says that "all have sinned and come short of the glory of God." God loves you, but He hates your sin because He is a God of unchanging holiness.

And God's justice never changes. Modern man likes to forget the justice of God. We like to think that the God of wrath is an illusion, a figment of the imagination of ancient writers. But I'm here to declare that the Bible from one end to the other declares God is going to judge the world and that you are going to be at the judgment.

In Deuteronomy 32 the Scripture says, "All his ways are judgment . . . just and right is he." Nobody's going to stand at the judgment and say, "Lord, You're wrong. You made a mistake. You're not just." The Bible says every knee will bow and every tongue will confess God's justice.

That's the reason I fear the judgment of God. I fear

justice. If Billy Graham gets justice, Billy Graham is lost. I have sinned against God. I have broken His law. What I want from God is mercy. I want His love. And I have found it in the Person of Jesus Christ. When I gave my life to Christ, the fear of going to hell left me. I know that I'm going to heaven because it depends completely on Christ. When He bowed His head on the cross and said, "It is finished," the provision of my salvation was complete and I can sing with the hymn writer, "Complete in Thee."

The Bible teaches that God hates sin so much that He sent His Son Jesus Christ to die on that cross. And the Bible says that those who persist in rejecting Jesus, living their own life the way they want to without regard to God, are going to be judged. The Bible says, "The soul that sinneth, it shall die." The Bible says the wicked shall be turned into hell, and all the nations that forget God.

The Scriptures tell us God judged the angels who sinned. The angels, the mighty angels of God, rebelled against Him, led by Lucifer, Son of the Morning. Lucifer must have been the highest of all created beings. He was God's anointed cherub. He apparently defended the throne of heaven. He was in charge of vast segments of the universe, and he led a rebellion against God. Isaiah, chapter 14, tells us his sin was selfishness and pride. He said, "I want to be like the most high God. I want to sit on God's throne. I want to be God." And the Bible says God banished him and the angels who followed him into outer darkness, and some day, the Bible says, God is going to cast them into the hell which was prepared for the devil and his angels. If God hated rebellion and sin so much that He would cast out angels from His presence, do you think that you and I are going to escape the judgment of God?

The Bible teaches that God did not spare His chosen people Israel from judgment. The sovereign God chose Israel to be His special people, but when they sinned and complained and disobeyed He judged them time after time. And when they turned away to other gods He allowed them to become slaves of the Babylonians. God judged His own people.

Our Bible passage says that God also judged the people of Noah's day. God saw that they continually did evil, and He sent the greatest flood in history and everybody perished except eight people. Noah warned the people to repent of their sins, but they mocked him. And one day the flood came. The people began to beat on the closed door of the ark, but Noah had secured the door. It was too late.

God judged the great cities of Canaan's productive plain for their sexual perversion. I don't know whether it was as bad as we have now, but it was so bad that God told Lot, a nephew of Abraham living in Sodom, "Get out," and then God rained fire and brimstone on Sodom and Gomorrah, destroying them.

Further, God judged His own servants. Look at Samson. He was chosen and anointed of the Lord. As long as he lived for God his strength was tremendous. But sin entered the picture. Samson began to play around with women and he forgot that the source of his strength was God. God judged him, and his enemies overcame him and put out his eyes and forced him to turn a mill wheel like a mule. Samson, the mighty man of God, suffered God's judgment.

The greatest judgment of all, the Bible says, fell upon God's own Son. He "spared not his Son, but delivered him up for us all," says Romans 8. God loved His Son. I cannot explain the Trinity: God the Father, God the Son, God the Holy Spirit — equal, united, and separate — but I accept it as a revelation from the Bible. God loved His Son above all creatures in the universe, but He also loved humanity, and the Bible says God gave His Son to judgment by deliberate plan. Christ, dying on the cross, said, "My God, why hast thou forsaken me?" And in that moment something happened that none of us can understand. God took your sins, and put them on Jesus Christ. And the cross became a judgment. Isaiah says our Redeemer was smitten of God. Peter says, "He did no sin; neither was guile found in his mouth. Who his own self bear our sins in his own body on the tree that we . . . should live unto righteousness." And Paul said in 2 Corinthians, "He hath made him to be sin for us." God the Father caused Jesus the Son to take your hell on that cross.

If you're willing to accept this truth, God will forgive your sins, write your name in His book in heaven and give you a new life here and now!

But some ask, "Will God spare America?" God didn't spare the ancients. He didn't spare Israel. He didn't spare Sodom and Gomorrah. He didn't spare His own servants and He didn't spare His own sinless Son. God didn't spare Germany, the cradle of the Reformation that became the slaughterhouse of the Jews.

Our beloved America is in trouble today. We're in trouble economically. We're in trouble racially. We're in trouble morally. We're in trouble with crime. No, I don't think God will spare America unless we have a national revival, a national repentance of our sins, and a national turning to God. We're a great nation, the greatest attempt at democracy in the history of the world, but God sees hearts filled with materialism, our surfeiting, our drunkenness, our immorality, our crime, our lawlessness, and our rebellion. We are very much like the degraded nations and cities of the past. But the judgment of God is held back for now by the people who trust in Him.

The Day of Judgment is coming. Will God spare you? The Bible says in Job 21, "The wicked is reserved to the day of destruction." Ecclesiastes 12 says, "God shall bring every work into judgment, with every secret thing, whether it be good or whether it be evil." In Matthew 12 Jesus said, "Every idle word that men shall speak, they shall give account in the Day of Judgment." In Acts 17 the Apostle Paul said God commands all men everywhere to repent, because He has appointed a day in which He will judge the world.

Do you want to hear a description of it? Revelation 20: 11 says: "Then I saw a large white throne and the one who sits on it. Earth and heaven fled from his presence, and were seen no more. And I saw the dead, great and small alike, standing before the throne. Books were opened, and then another book was opened, the book of the living. The dead were judged according to what they had done, as was written in the books. Then the sea gave up its dead. Death and the world of the dead also gave up the dead they held. And all were judged according to what they had done. Then death and the world of the dead were thrown into the lake of fire. (This lake of fire is the second death.) Whoever did not have his name written in the book of the living was thrown into the lake of fire."

These are not the words of Billy Graham. Whatever God means by the "lake of fire," there's a judgment coming. Something deep inside of us tells us that judgment is coming. Are you ready?

You say, "What do I have to do?"

You have to be willing to repent of your sin and receive Christ into your heart. You see, Jesus took your judgment on the cross, and if you will receive Him, by faith, your judgment is passed. Today you may be standing at the crossroads of your life. The Bible says, "He that hardeneth his heart, being often reproved, shall suddenly be cut off, and that without remedy." The Bible says today is the day of salvation, and in Noah's day God said, "My Spirit shall not always strive with men." You can come to Christ only when the Spirit of God enables you, and the Spirit of God is speaking to you right now.

You may be Catholic, Protestant, or Jewish. You may not have any religion at all. You may be a church member or you may not go to any church, but if you know you need Christ and you repent of your sin, then receive Him by faith and your name will be written in the book of life. "Believe on the Lord Jesus Christ," the Bible says, "and thou shall be saved."

20

The Not Too Late Show

Does televising the Crusades influence people? Is it worthwhile?

Perhaps we should ask the ranger at Cottonwood Ranger Station, thirty-five miles from Indio, California. Monday night at the Anaheim Crusade he and his wife came forward to make public a television commitment made in their home in the wilds at Chiriaco Summit in June 1969. While watching the New York Crusade on television, this ranger and his wife felt the impact of Billy Graham's message and together trusted Christ. When they learned of the Anaheim Crusade the distance seemed short.

Or we might ask the father of a family from Walnut Creek near San Francisco what he thinks of televising the Billy Graham Crusades. Tuesday night at the Crusade, advisor Dick Murray, new associate pastor in Orange, was handed a counselor's card and introduced to a young girl. He paused to read the card and then turned in surprise to the girl. "What in the world are you doing down here from Walnut Creek?"

Smiling, she answered, "Dad and Mom are new Christians and so are we kids. We all accepted Christ as a result of watching a Billy Graham Crusade on TV. Dad wanted to make sure all was well for the family, so he packed us all in the car and we drove down just for this Crusade."

Dick Murray was astonished. He had just left a pastorate in Walnut Creek. Out of the thousands of people he could have advised that evening, he should be introduced to this girl! The young lady found her family and introduced them to her advisor. The father's desire was that his family become established in a Bible-believing church in Walnut Creek. Who could give him better advice than Dick Murray! Dick was still shaking his head as the family walked away smiling and waving.

We might ask the woman from Tustin what the televised Crusade did for her. She had attended the Crusade nightly without her husband, an avowed atheist. Later she wanted to watch the 11 P.M telecast but found herself unable to stay awake. Leaving her husband at the TV, she said, "Will you wake me at 11 so I can watch the Billy Graham Crusade?" He promised he would.

Shortly before the program he tried waking her. She murmured sleepily and drifted back to sleep. Her husband set up his tape recorder to capture the program for her. Sometime later, as she explains it, she woke up and heard her husband sobbing. Only once before had she known him to cry.

She got out of bed and went to him. He was completely unnerved. George Beverly Shea had sung, "How Great Thou Art," the favorite song of his mother who had recently died. The wife comforted him, thanked him for his thoughtfulness in taping Billy's message, and communicated her feelings about Christ as she'd never done before. "There's a crack in his spiritual armor now," she told a friend. "For the first time he's going to church with me and isn't scoffing — pray for him!"

Peggy, a Garden Grove coed who attends Cal State College, attended the Crusade and heard Billy speak on heaven and hell. She came at the invitation of a friend who accepted Christ the first night of the Crusade. But Peggy, with her long braids, Indian head band, beads, bangles and bracelets, didn't respond. She was "hung-up" on self-realization and reincarnation. Her friend suggested that she watch the televised meetings after the Crusade, and Peggy did. The next day she told her friend, "That TV program did it! Would you believe I gave my heart to Jesus!"

Letters reach the Billy Graham Evangelistic Association office in Minneapolis regularly, telling of the televised Crusade's impact on lives. Letters such as this: "My husband made a commitment to Christ at Madison Square Garden when you were there. I was unable to attend as I am a partial invalid, but I watched the services on television and I want to make a commitment to Christ also."

Another said: "We want to thank you for coming into our home via TV. I can honestly say that I have never been so inspired, even though I am a church member, to trust the Lord and become as a child of God. I no longer am anxious for tomorrow. I now begin each day by asking God to help me accept His will, whatever He has planned for me, and guide me in the direction He wants me to go. I cannot begin to tell you how this has helped me. . . ."

A letter from a lady states she was watching a televised Crusade service while standing at her ironing board, and she turned her life over the Lord. Another came from a would-be suicide. Letters come from children and adults, from all walks of life, and every state in the union.

The first night the Anaheim Crusade was telecast in Arizona a call came through to the Crusade office and Don Myers was summoned to deal with the caller.

The fellow's name was Ben. He said he was an alcoholic, and what he had just seen and heard on TV showed him he needed help. His question was, "What do I do now?"

Don led him carefully through the plan of salvation, then said, "I want to say a prayer of invitation for Jesus Christ to come into your life and turn your life around. You listen to the prayer and then if you understand it and want to pray it afterward, that's fine."

Don began the prayer, phrase by phrase, but he hadn't gone far when the man started saying it after him — he just couldn't wait, he told Don. He both understood what his need was and knew where to find help.

There is criticism of some TV appearances, too. Many Christians questioned Billy's visits on the sometimes irreverent "Laugh-In" and "Woody Allen" shows. But some positive benefits are evident.

A counselor asked a 19-year-old sandal-clad youth at the Anaheim Crusade, "Why did you come forward tonight?" "It wasn't the sermon," the young man said. "I saw Billy on the Woody Allen Show and I heard him say Christ was helping him right then. If He can do that for a man on the Woody Allen Show, that's the Christ I want." This hippie had flown from San Francisco to Los Angeles and responded when the invitation was given at the Crusade. He is planning to study for the ministry.

Billy offers this explanation. "I am told by a group of 'far-outers' that appearances on popular television shows had made it the 'in' thing to come to the Anaheim Crusade. They said the stigma of going to a religious meeting has been removed. Jesus was criticized by the religious leaders of His day for spending too much time with publicans and outcasts. His strategy was to go where they were in order to reach them, without compromising with their evil deeds.

"This was also the strategy of Paul. He said in 1 Corinthians 9:20-22, 'While working with the Jews, I live like a Jew in order to win them; and even though I myself am not subject to the Law of Moses, I live as though I were, when working with those who are, in order to win them. In the same way I live like a Gentile, outside the Jewish Law, in order to win Gentiles. This does not mean that I do not obey God's law, for I am really under Christ's law. Among the weak in the faith, I become weak like one of them, in order to win them. So I become all things to all men, that I may save some of them by any means possible.' In other words, the Apostle Paul would try to win 'common ground' with those to whom he was witnessing.

"Sometimes this is not easy. I am one of the few evangelical clergymen that has invitations to appear on such programs. My purpose in going is twofold. One is to give a witness, and the other is to find common ground with our materialistic and secularistic society in order to witness more effectively. Sometimes I am put in rather delicate situations, and I need your prayers for wisdom. You can be sure we will never accept an invitation unless we can bear a witness for Christ."

The Anaheim Crusade was nationally televised at a cost of about $1 million. Yet the Graham organization feels TV is one of the most productive and efficient means for proclaiming the Gospel. A letter from a Jewish mother to network officials illustrates the point.

"As a Jewish mother of three who have impressionable minds and who sat down to watch 'Laugh-In' the other night, I was shocked to hear a missionary message given by Billy Graham at the end of the program. . . . NBC had no right to put over on an unsuspecting public hidden persuaders for Christianity . . . have you turned into a propaganda agency?"

Christians pray the three children *were* impressed — more impressed by John 3:16 which Mr. Graham quoted than by the off-color jokes that are the usual fare on that program. Billy touched the audience he aimed for — those who never enter a church or come to a Crusade. It is one way of becoming "all things to all men" — and women — to win some. By TV antennae, Billy proclaims the saving Gospel of Christ "from the housetops."

21

Billy in for the Angels

An earnest woman met Ruth Graham and said plaintively, "I've always wished I could shake your husband's hand before I die!" Ruth Graham, smiling, answered, "Sometimes I feel the same way!"

Everyone laughed. If there is one wife who is close to her husband though he is thousands of miles away, it is Ruth Graham. It was the last Sunday afternoon of the Anaheim Crusade, and soon Ruth Graham would be able to take her Bill home, at least for a short while.

For the third time within a week, the stadium attendance record was broken. The afternoon service brought the cumulative attendance to 384,000 and total decisions to 20,-336. More people responded to the appeal to receive Christ in the ten days at Anaheim than in any similar period in Billy's ministry. Dr. Wirt, editor of *Decision* magazine, remarked, "I've never been to a Crusade where I've seen such spiritual excitement and where everyone appears almost to be on tiptoe!"

Billy confided to a friend: "Many of these people were so prepared before the Crusade by the Holy Spirit that I feel they'd have come forward if I had just gotten up and quoted John 3:16; this clearly demonstrates the power of prayer."

During the baseball season a disillusioned sports writer had lamented: "What the Angels need is a pinch-hitter like Billy Graham. He's about the only one who can fill that stadium." To even hint that a religious service could do what the great American sport could not do was unthinkable. Yet it became fact.

Billy had been compared to a baseball pitcher in an unofficial aside at the dedication service preceding the Crusade. Team member Willis Haymaker had predicted: "We're going to see some fastballs right over the plate when Billy comes." Certainly Billy's pitches were straight and hard, the kind that keen eyes would pick out and translate into home runs. Pitches like this:

"Jesus Christ never promised life would be easy. . . . But I've a feeling that American young people will respond to the challenge of Christ if we will tell it like it is."

"If you come to Christ you've got to be willing to be different — to be a nonconformist. The Bible says our bodies are to be the temple of the Holy Spirit; we are to present them as living sacrifices to Christ."

"What does it mean to take up the cross and follow Christ? It means you are willing to share the reproach of Christ and willing to let the world laugh at you, willing to live a separated life — a life of discipline, of Bible reading and study and prayer. It means you are willing to speak with a tongue that has been crucified, willing to redeem the time no matter what the cost. If you are willing to lose this life for His sake, you gain not only this life but the life to come."

"People who have real peace, joy and fulfillment are the people who are willing to lose their life for Christ's sake. What shall it profit a man if he gain the whole world but lose his own soul? I ask you to exchange your life for Jesus Christ's."

The shadow of triple-tiered Angel Stadium was beginning to curtain the lower infield when the last "Amen" was sung by the choir and a hushed crowd began leaving the stadium. It was hard to believe that the wonder days were ended, that throngs of spectators would no longer be transformed into participants by converging on the Angels playing field, that Billy Graham would drop from the newspapers' front pages. Was it really all over?

That final Sunday, the Crusade bulletin carried a message from Billy Graham that asked: "Is This the End?" He answered by saying: "Calendar-wise, this is the last day of the Crusade. However, it is not the end, but rather the beginning. What God does is always continuing, for He works in the dimension of eternity. The Scripture, 'I give unto them eternal life, and no man shall pluck them out of my hand,' has no terminal date on it, and what has started in many hearts will outlive the stars and outshine the sun.

"What has happened at Anaheim Stadium? Some cynical souls may say, 'Nothing.' They shrug their shoulders and pass it off as a carnival of emotion, as a conclave where evangelicals reconfirm their beliefs, and as a fellowship-fest. I concede that the Crusade during these days has evoked some emotion, if by that word you mean heartfelt enthusiasm and concern about things that really matter. I even wish there had been much more. Although I have never tried to generate emotion, people feel very deeply when the Spirit of God moves, and I would that the Church could generate more warmth and fire.

"Yes, there has been Christian fellowship. The Bible says, 'If we walk in the light as he is in the light, we have fellowship one with another.' If nothing more happened here than thousands singing together, praying together, and working together as a witness to Christian solidarity, it would all have been worthwhile.

"And I must confess that we are guilty as charged, that this has been a time when Christians reconfirm their beliefs. In all our Crusades, quite a large percentage of those coming forward are already members of a church. Even in the first century, John wrote in Revelation, 'I have something against thee because thou hast left thy first love.' In no area of life must we guard more carefully against coldness and indifference. The Christian life requires discipline and dedication, and there are times when it is appropriate for Christians to reaffirm their faith in Christ. Many have done this, and for this we are grateful. That was one of the prime objectives of the Crusade.

"But I believe much more has happened. Jesus said that when the Gospel is preached, miracles happen, lives are changed, people pass from darkness to light. When I have given the appeal and people have come forward in the Crusade, it isn't my hypnotic eye, the tone of voice or the singing of the choir that makes them come. It is the wooing and persuasion of the Holy Spirit of God. Jesus said that when the Gospel is preached, if He be lifted up, all men will be drawn to Him, and we have witnessed this indescribable occurrence from night to night. This happens wherever and whenever the Gospel is preached with fervency and sincerity.

"But where do we go from here? Is this the end? Is the Crusade over? If it is — it really shouldn't have begun. Let us go out of the stadium as an army of compassion. Let us march not in some spectacular parade, protesting something or other, but proclaiming Christ and His love as the answer to deepest human need. If the millions of Christians across the world would dare to demonstrate the love of Christ in every area of their lives, some of the alarming trends we see could well be reversed.

"Let us go back to our homes with a new dedication, with a new discipline, to pray, to live Christ and, as the Bible says, to be seen and read of all men. And when we do, and I pray we will, this Crusade will have just begun. God bless you."

Numerous signs indicated that something wonderful was just beginning. The Holy Spirit who empowered Billy Graham remained in Anaheim, and in post-crusade days His power began appearing in countless lives up and down the California coast.

22

The Beginning

The folding machine in the Crusade office at Anaheim Stadium had pitched out its last letter, and the last envelope had been typed and stuffed. The office had moved out of the maze of cubicles and the large room where thousands of volunteers invested thousands of hours into two small offices that would be maintained for six months.

As the post-crusade phase began, the telephones started ringing afresh. Letters arrived and doorbells buzzed. Counselors, advisors, and ministers were following up on inquirers. Personal visits were made, and inquirers responded.

A teenager wrote to her counselor: "I'd better reintroduce myself. I'm Betty, the girl you counseled during the Billy Graham Crusade. I wanted to thank you for your most encouraging words that night. You made me really feel wanted and needed by the Lord. It's only been a week since the Crusade, when I gave my commitment to Christ, but so much has happened. My faith has tripled and I really feel full of Jesus Christ. Everywhere I go, I see the beauty God created and my faith is strengthened in seeing God's power at work, because it was His doing, in really coming into my heart. I've been a churchgoer all my life, but I was playing a role. Now it's *real.* I thank you for being a part of my reawakening. May God bless and take care of the truly lovely Christians such as you."

Evangelistic organizations such as Youth for Christ set to work on the counseling cards. The names of high school and college-age young people were taken off, to be given to Christian students for follow-up contacts.

Telephone counseling proceeded without interruption after the Crusade ended. Team members and office staff were on hand. On one occasion Co-Labor Chief Myers received a call from a hysterical woman in San Diego who said, "I don't have anything to live for; I'm going to commit suicide . . ." Don talked to her until she quieted down and would listen. He told her God loved her and Christ wanted to give her a reason for living. Finally she prayed with Don to receive Christ. She enrolled in a Bible correspondence course and has been sending in assignments regularly.

Many churches in the area reported exciting, wonderful days after the Crusade. Sunday school and church attendance increased. A church which took hundreds of people on buses from housing tracts to the Crusade has since drawn many people to neighborhood Bible studies.

A story that came to light after the Crusade pointed the way to bridging today's generation gap. A teenage girl with no church background came alone to one of the meetings because she was curious about Billy Graham — and because she had deep problems. She heard Billy declare that God through Christ has provided the answer to all of man's needs, and she went forward and asked Christ to be her Savior.

She also invited her counselor to come to her home and visit her mother, who was very ill. The counselor brought along a friend who was a gracious visitor to sick people. They found the mother, in her mid-forties, slowly dying of cancer. She couldn't speak, had lost all her hair and a great deal of weight. The counselor's friend explained slowly and simply to the dying woman what had happened to her daughter at the Crusade, and then told her of the love of God and sacrifice of Christ for our sins. As she spoke, the mother watched her intently, tears sliding down her cheeks.

The visitor asked the woman to indicate in some way if she understood, and then prayed for her. When the prayer was finished, the dying woman looked up and said, "Thank you." She had not spoken for many weeks, nor did she speak again after that. A few days later she died. With the ending of her life on this earth came the beginning of spiritual life for the rest of the family, as the father and six other children also placed their faith in Christ.

And what was happening to biker Rick? Counselor John McMullin wrote to him from Canada: "It was great to talk with you on the telephone the other night and to hear about your growth as a Christian. I have had the opportunity to speak to many people about a personal relationship with Jesus Christ, but I believe God brought you and me together for a special purpose. My life will never be the same again and my faith in Him has been increased as I witnessed your life being completely changed in direction. You learned so quickly that it was not a matter of having to give up things but obtaining something much more desirable than what you had before. I think the Bible expresses it much more adequately in the Testament I gave to you, as follows: 'When someone becomes a Christian he becomes a brand new person inside. He is not the same any more. A new life has begun!' (2 Corinthians 5:17) . . . This is just a brief note to let you know that we are thinking about you and we pray for you daily. . . . Your brother in Christ, John."

Lionel Mayell made several calls at Rick's home and completed arrangements for him to stay at Campus Crusade for Christ headquarters in Arrowhead Springs above San Bernadino where he could get a job and receive training in the Christian life. Lionel confirmed: "God has done a fantastic job in Rick's life."

The change was dramatic indeed. The first Monday night of the Crusade I had stumbled across the opening scene of the drama. On coming down to the field from the press box after the service, I observed a woman dabbing at her eyes, her cheeks glistening with tears. I approached her and asked if she needed some help. Swallowing hard, she said, "This is a very crucial night for me. That's my son over there . . ." and she pointed to Rick. She related to me something of Rick's life and her deep anxiety. Then we prayed together. As we parted she handed me her business card and we agreed to keep in touch. I went back up to the Co-Labor office and shared the story, and many people began praying for Rick. In subsequent nights, and days, the transforming events occurred as described in Chapter 6.

Following the Crusade I made a trip to the valley where Rick lives to hear his story. Since then Rick and his mother have been guests in our home, and it is, as Billy Graham stated, a continuing story, for what God does has eternal dimensions.

At this writing Rick is witnessing with Campus Crusade for Christ in schools near San Bernardino. He has been instrumental in leading several biker friends to the Lord. On one visit he greeted me with: "Hey, guess what! Three more of my biker partners are going to heaven with me!"

One of his best biker buddies was shooting cocaine which, as Rick said, has killed fellows who have been on it two months. Rick took him out to lunch and related all that had happened to him. The friend invited Christ into his life, and Rick reported confidently: "Even if he dies right now from the effects of the cocaine, he's going to heaven because he really did receive Christ into his heart."

Rick becomes reflective now and then. "I thank the Lord every day for two things," he revealed, "that my mom, even though she saw the things I did and the way I looked, continued to pray for me and she let me know she loved me; and that the Lord has a plan for my life that He is revealing to me."

His copy of *The Living New Testament* was so marked up within a week that you'd guess he had been using it for years. Rick planned to get copies for his nieces and nephews and then to "sit down and have Bible study with them"!

How many more transformations will issue from the Anaheim Crusade must be recorded by the angels above. But I think the Christians of southern California will be rejoicing with the angels for a long time to come!

A final word, please, to readers whose lives were transformed by the Anaheim Crusade — a word from the Word: "And I am sure that God who began the good work within you will keep right on helping you grow in His grace until His task within you is finally finished on that day when Jesus Christ returns" (Philippians 1:6, *The Living New Testament*).